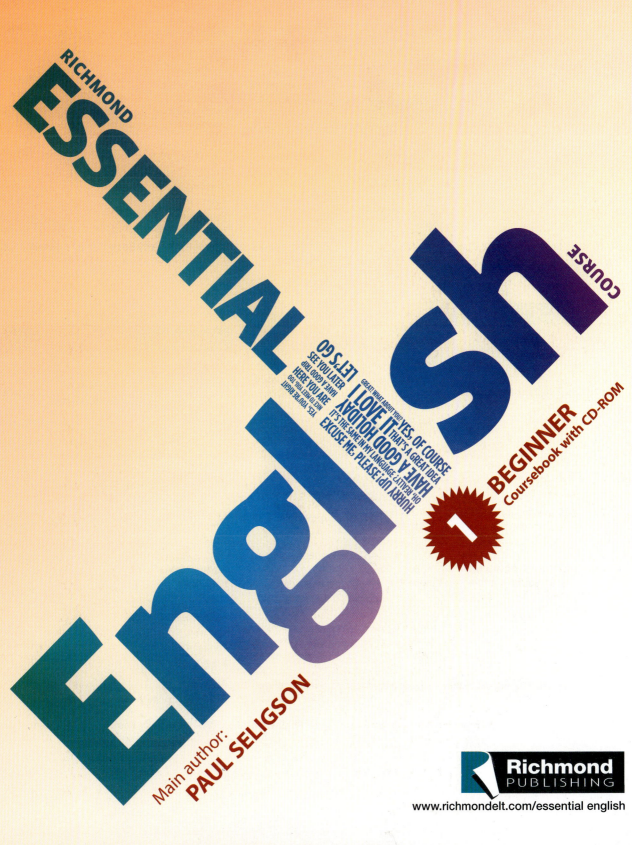

RICHMOND

# ESSENTIAL English

COURSE

YES, OF COURSE
GREAT! WHAT ABOUT YOU?
THAT'S A GREAT IDEA
I LOVE IT!
OH, REALLY?
HAVE A GOOD HOLIDAY
IT'S THE SAME IN MY LANGUAGE
HURRY UP!
EXCUSE ME, PLEASE
LET'S GO
SEE YOU LATER
HAVE A GOOD TRIP
HERE YOU ARE
NICE TO MEET YOU, TOO
YES, YOU'RE RIGHT

1 BEGINNER
Coursebook with CD-ROM

Main author:
PAUL SELIGSON

Richmond PUBLISHING
www.richmondelt.com/essential english

# Contents

# 1A Nice to meet you!

The Green Park Hotel

OPENING PARTY!

## Listening

**1** (1.1) Listen. Complete the dialogue.

| | |
|---|---|
| **Leo:** | Hi. |
| **Anna:** | Hello. |
| **Leo:** | I'm Leo. |
| **Anna:** | Hi, Leo. My name's ________. Nice to meet you. |
| **Leo:** | Nice to meet you, too. |

**2** Listen again and repeat.

**3** Say hello to your classmates.

A: *Hi, I'm ... .*

B: *Hello, ... . My name's ... .*

A: *Nice ... .*

B: *... .*

**4** (1.2) Match the words and photos. Listen and repeat.

an actor   a book   a city   a party   a restaurant   ~~a supermarket~~   a TV programme

1 *a supermarket*

2 ______________

3 ______________

4 ______________

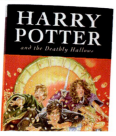

HARRY POTTER and the Deathly Hallows

5 ______________

6 ______________

7 ______________

## Grammar

**5** Look at the Grammar box. Complete 1–4 with *a* or *an*.

1 *a* hotel
2 ___ airport
3 ___ film
4 ___ exercise

| Indefinite article |
|---|
| **a** book |
| **an** actor |

**6** Look at Exercise 4 again. Cover the words and test yourself with the photos.

## Listening

**7** 1.3 Listen. Are Anna and Leo positive (+) or negative (–)?

**8** Listen again. Circle the words you hear.

| | |
|---|---|
| **Anna:** | *Wow!* / *Yuck!* It's a *fantastic* / *terrible* party! |
| **Leo:** | *Yes!* / *No!* And the food is *good* / *bad*, too. |
| **Anna:** | Mmm! *Yes* / *No*, I agree! |
| **Leo:** | And *a* / *the* Green Park's an *excellent* / *OK* hotel! |

## Grammar

**9** 1.4 Order the adjectives in the box from positive to negative. Listen, check and repeat.

good excellent terrible OK

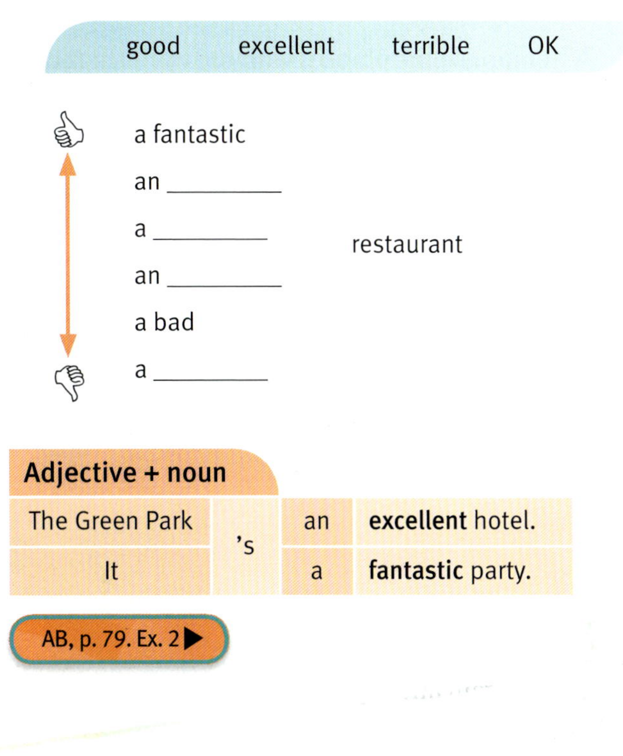


| Adjective + noun | | | |
|---|---|---|---|
| The Green Park | 's | an | **excellent** hotel. |
| It | | a | **fantastic** party. |

AB, p. 79. Ex. 2 ▶

## Speaking

**10** Look at the Grammar box. Write *a* or *an* in the blue circles. In pairs, say five sentences.

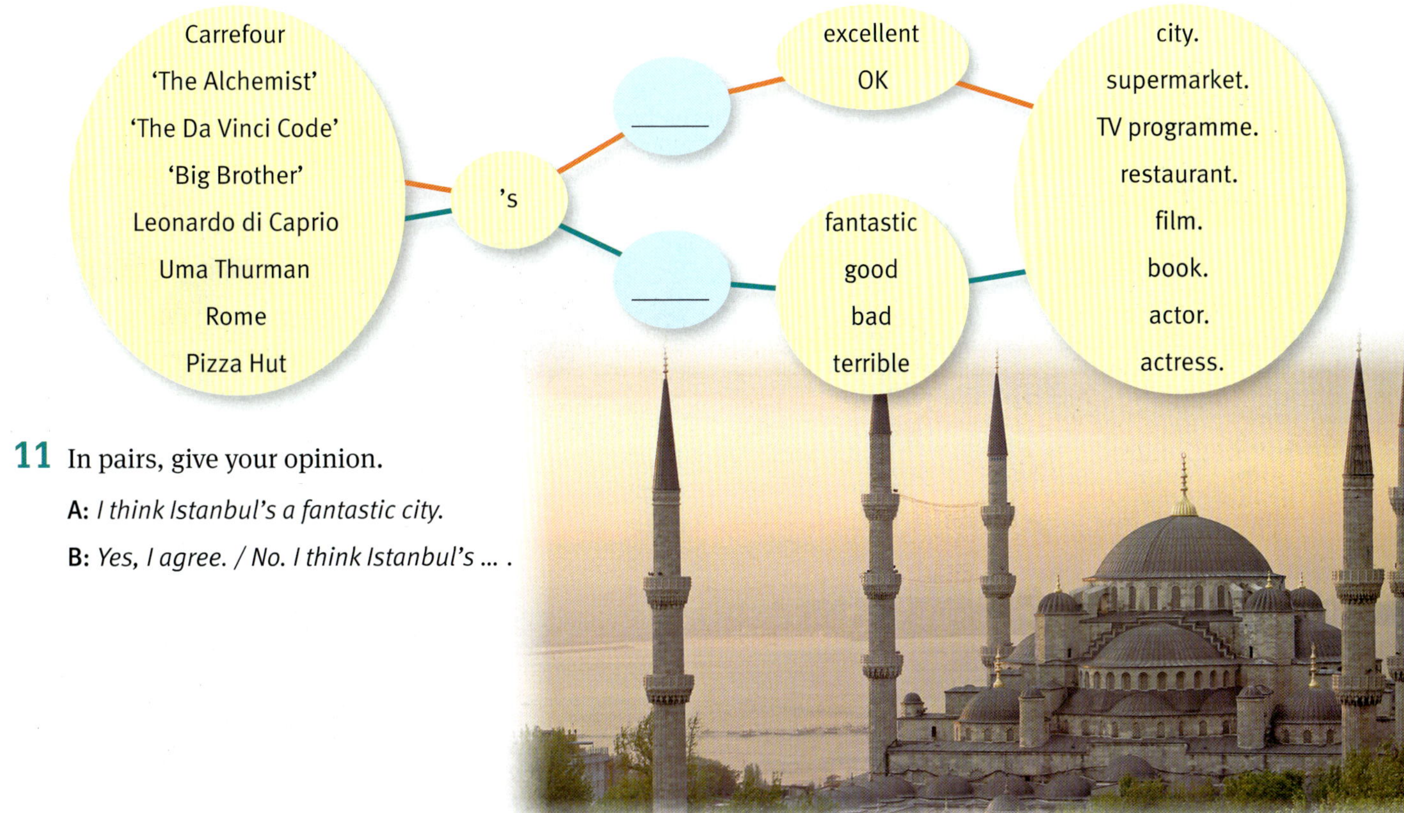


**11** In pairs, give your opinion.

**A:** *I think Istanbul's a fantastic city.*

**B:** *Yes, I agree. / No. I think Istanbul's ... .*

# 1B I'm fine, thanks

## Speaking

**1** 1.5 Say 1–12 in English. Word Bank 1A, p. 64.

**2** 1.6 Complete the phrases with the words in the box. Listen, check and repeat.

> Good ~~Goodbye~~ morning night you

**Say hello**

1 to 12.00 p.m. → Good ________.

2 12.00 p.m. to 6.00 p.m. → ________ afternoon.

3 6.00 p.m. → Good evening.

**Say goodbye**

4 *Goodbye*.

5 See ________. Bye.

6 6.00 p.m. → Good ________.

**3** Say hello to your classmates.

## Listening

**4** 1.7 Listen. Complete the dialogue with the words in the box.

> you And is I'm evening this

| | |
|---|---|
| **Kate:** | Good evening. |
| **Leo:** | Good (1) ________. |
| **Kate:** | Are you Leo? Leo Jackson? |
| **Leo:** | Yes, I am, (2) ________ you're ... Sorry, I don't remember. What's your name? |
| **Kate:** | (3) ________ Kate. Kate Dixon. |
| **Leo:** | Right! How are you, Kate? |
| **Kate:** | I'm fine, thanks. And (4) ________? |
| **Leo:** | I'm fine, too. Oh, I'm sorry ... Kate, this (5) ________ Anna. Anna, (6) ________ is Kate. |
| **Anna:** | Hello, Kate. |
| **Kate:** | Hi. Nice to meet you, Anna. |

**5** Listen and repeat. In pairs, practise the dialogue.

**6** In groups, introduce people.

**Lars:** *Clara, this is Carlos. Carlos, this is Clara.*

**Clara:** *Hello, Carlos. Nice to meet you.*

**Carlos:** *Hi. Nice to meet you, too.*

## Grammar

**7** Look at the dialogue in Exercise 4 again. Complete the Grammar box.

**Verb *be***

| + | − |
|---|---|
| I ______ Kate.<br>You**'re** Leo. | I**'m not** Anna.<br>You **aren't** Lars. |

| ? | ✓/✗ |
|---|---|
| ______ you Leo? | Yes, I ______.<br>No, I**'m not**. |

**Contractions**
I'm = I am
you're = you are
aren't = are not

AB, p. 80. Ex. 1 ▶

**8** Say hello to your classmates again. Remember all the names!

**A:** *Are you ...?*

**B:** *Yes, I am. / No, I'm not. I'm ... and you're ... (Sorry, I don't remember.)*

**A:** *How are you, ...? / I'm ... .*

**B:** *I'm ..., thanks. And you?*

**A:** *I'm ... .*

## Pronunciation

**9** (1.8) Listen and repeat the sound and words.

| /aɪ/ | hi | five | nice | night |
|---|---|---|---|---|
| /ɪ/ | it | this | six | aspirin |

**10** (1.9) Say the phrases. Listen and repeat.

H**i**, **I**'m f**i**ne!

a n**i**ce n**i**ght

Th**i**s f**i**lm **i**s terr**i**ble!

Th**i**nk **i**n **E**ngl**i**sh!

## Classroom English

**11** (1.10) Listen. Match the dialogues and the pictures. Listen again and repeat.

**A**

**Teacher:** OK, class? Please look at page 11.

**Lars:** Oops, I'm sorry! Just a moment.

**Teacher:** Lars. Are you OK?

**Lars:** Yes, I'm fine thanks.

**B**

**Teacher:** Come in.

**Lars:** Sorry, I'm late.

**Teacher:** That's OK, Lars.

**12** (1.11) What classroom instructions do you know? Word Bank 2, p. 65.

# What's this in English?

## Classroom English

**1** 1.12 Match the words and objects in the picture. Listen, check and repeat.

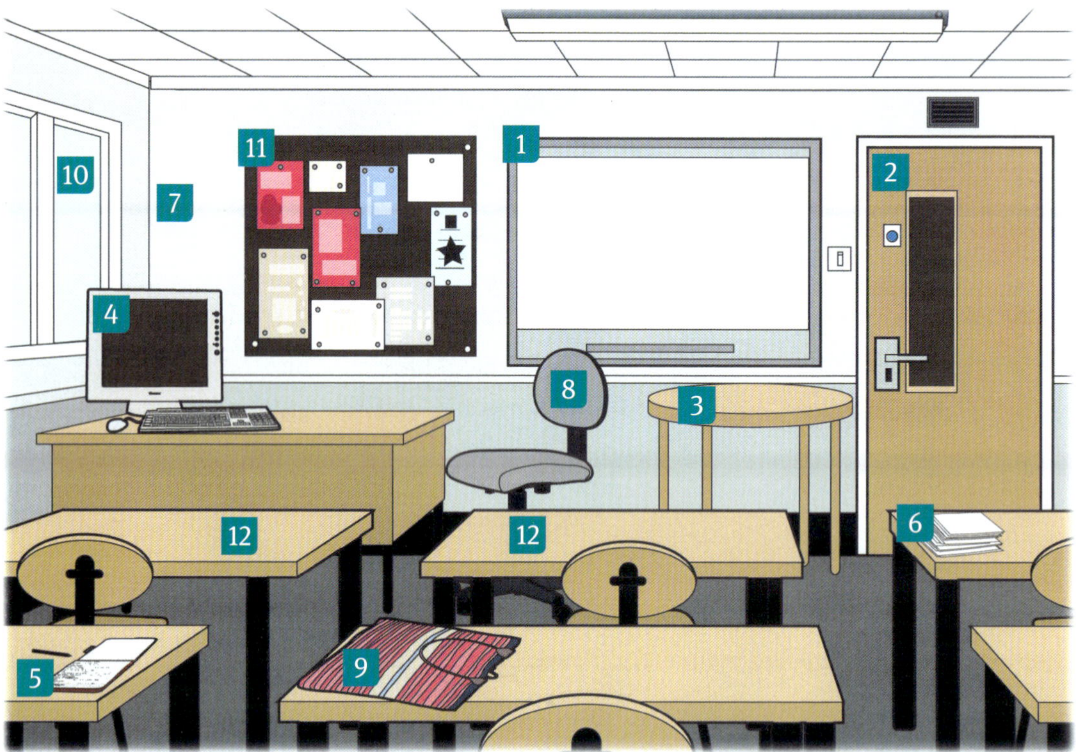

a bag ___

a board ___

a chair ___

a computer ___

desks ___

a door ___

a notebook ___

a noticeboard ___

sheets of paper ___

a table ___

walls ___

a window ___

**2** Say all the words in Exercise 1 in the plural.

**3** Play I CAN SEE. What can you see in your classroom?

A: *I can see (twelve) desks.*

B: *And I can see a computer.*

**Tip**

Common plurals: noun + *s*

**a word → words**

**a photo → photos**

**4** 1.13 Match dialogues 1 and 2 to pictures A and B. Listen, check and repeat.

1

| | |
|---|---|
| **Lars:** | What's this in English? |
| **Teacher:** | It's a chair. |
| **Lars:** | And what are these? |
| **Teacher:** | They're CD-ROMs. |
| **Lars:** | Thank you. |
| **Teacher:** | You're welcome. |

2

| | |
|---|---|
| **Rita:** | Excuse me, please. |
| **Teacher:** | Yes? |
| **Rita:** | What's that? |
| **Teacher:** | It's a whiteboard. |
| **Rita:** | And what are those? |
| **Teacher:** | They're magazines. |

A ___

B ___

## Grammar

**5** Look at the pictures and dialogues in Exercise 4. Complete the Grammar box with the words in the box.

Is (×2) are (×2) Singular Plural Are (×2) it they

### Verb *be*

| | ____________ | ✓✗ |
|---|---|---|
| + | This **is** a desk. That**'s** a chair. | |
| ? | What**'s** this / that (in English)? | It**'s** a desk. It **isn't** a chair. |
| | ___ it a desk? | Yes, ___ **is**. |
| | ___ it a chair? | No, it **isn't**. |

| | ____________ | ✓✗ |
|---|---|---|
| + | These **are** CD-ROMs. Those ____ DVDs. | |
| ? | What **are** these / those (in English)? | They**'re** CD-ROMs. They **aren't** DVDs. |
| | ____ they CD-ROMs? | Yes, they ____. |
| | ____ they DVDs? | No, ______ **aren't**. |

**Contractions**

it's = it is they're = they are

isn't = is not aren't = are not

AB, p. 81. Ex. 1 ▶

## Pronunciation

**6** 1.14 Listen and repeat.

this these that those

**7** 1.15 Listen, chant and mime.

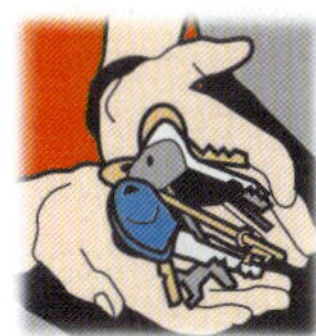

**8** 1.16 What's on your desk? Word Bank 3, p. 66.

**9** Look at the photos. Ask your teacher what they are.

**A:** *Photo number 1. Is it a diary?*

1 

2 

3 

4 

## Listening

**10** 1.17 Listen. Complete the dialogue.

**Lars:** What are (1) ____________ in English?

**Rita:** (2) ____________ keys. Are (3) ____________ newspapers?

**Lars:** No, no, I don't remember. (4) ____________ a moment. No. No, they (5) ____________. They aren't newspapers, they're ... (6) ____________.

**11** In pairs, ask and answer. Point to things in the classroom.

# Where are you from?

## Listening

**1** 1.18 Listen. Circle the correct option.

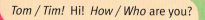

Sorry *I'm late!* / *to be late!*
*Tom* / *Tim!* Hi! *How* / *Who* are you?


**2** 1.19 Listen. Match the people and cities.

| | |
|---|---|
| 1 Tim | a York |
| 2 Anna | b Sydney |
| 3 Kate | c Milan |
| 4 Leo | d Washington |

**3** Listen again, read and repeat. In groups, practise the dialogue.

| | |
|---|---|
| **Tim:** | Where are you from, Kate? You aren't British ... |
| **Kate:** | No, I'm not. I'm from the USA, from Washington. And you? Where are you from? |
| **Tim:** | Guess! |
| **Kate:** | Hmmm, I don't know ... Are you from Australia? |
| **Tim:** | Yes, I am! I'm from Sydney. |
| **Kate:** | Where are you from, Anna? |
| **Anna:** | Me? I'm Italian. |
| **Leo:** | Really? Where in Italy are you from? |
| **Anna:** | I'm from Milan. And you? |
| **Leo:** | I'm from York. Not New York! York in England. I'm British. Your English is excellent, Anna. Congratulations! |
| **Anna:** | Oh ... Thank you. |

**4** 1.20 Complete the table with words from the dialogue. Listen, check and repeat.

| | | Country | Nationality |
|---|---|---|---|
| 1 | [Australian flag] | ______ | Australian |
| 2 | [Italian flag] | ______ | ______ |
| 3 | [British flag] | Britain | ______ |
| 4 | [US flag] | ______ | American |

## Grammar

**5** Look at the dialogue in Exercise 3 and complete the Grammar box.

**Verb *be* + nationalities**

| | | |
|---|---|---|
| **+** | | |
| I<br>You/We/They | 'm<br>___ | Australian.<br>from Australia. |
| **–** | | |
| I<br>You/We/They | 'm not<br>aren't | Italian.<br>from Italy. |
| **?** | | |
| ___ | you/we/they | American?<br>from the USA? |
| **✓/✗** | | |
| ✓ Yes, | I | ___. |
| | you/we/they | are. |
| ✗ No, | I'm | not. |
| | you/we/they | ___. |
| **?** | | |
| Where are you/we/they ___? | | |

**Contractions**

we're = we are

AB, p. 82. Ex. 3 ▶

**6** Ask where your classmates are from.

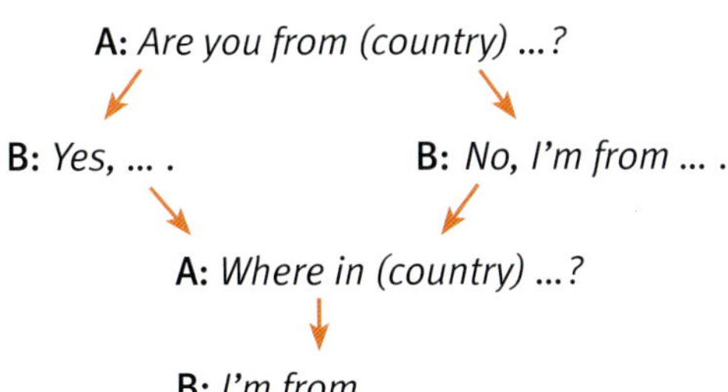


B: *No, I'm from ... .*
A: *Where in (country) ...?*

**Tip**

**CAPITAL LETTERS**
**I**taly – **I**talian

**Special plurals**
*consonant* + y → –y + ies
countr**y** → countr**ies**
nationalit**y** → nationalit**ies**

**7** 1.21 Name three more countries and nationalities. Word Bank 4, p. 67.

## Reading

**8** 1.22 Listen and read the text from a travel magazine. Circle the correct option.

1 England, Scotland, Wales and Northern Ireland *are / aren't* countries.
2 People from Wales are *English / British*.
3 Northern Ireland *is / isn't* a part of Britain.
4 Britain and England *are / aren't* the same country.

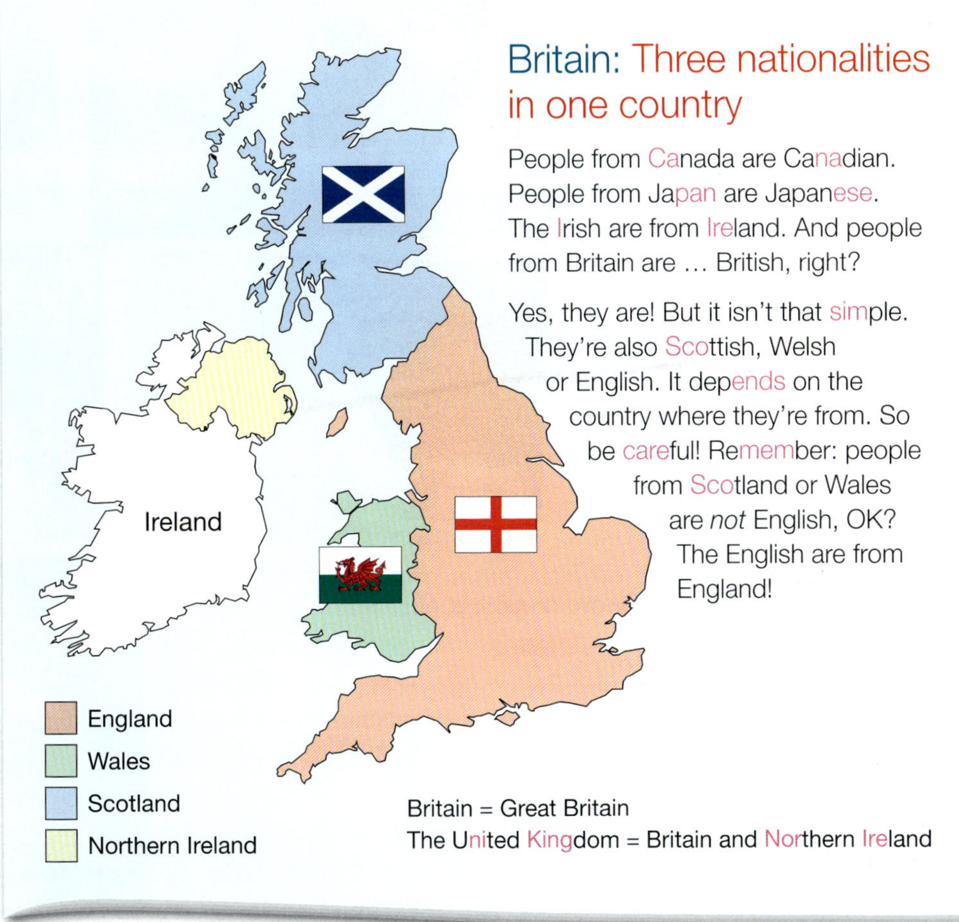

Britain: Three nationalities in one country
People from Canada are Canadian. People from Japan are Japanese. The Irish are from Ireland. And people from Britain are … British, right?
Yes, they are! But it isn't that simple. They're also Scottish, Welsh or English. It depends on the country where they're from. So be careful! Remember: people from Scotland or Wales are *not* English, OK? The English are from England!
Ireland
England
Wales
Scotland
Northern Ireland
Britain = Great Britain
The United Kingdom = Britain and Northern Ireland


**9** Cover the text and look at the picture. In pairs, remember and say the country and nationalities.

**A:** *This is England. They're ... .*

**10** Play GUESS THE COUNTRY.
Students A & B: choose a continent and a country.
Group: ask questions to guess the country.

**Group:** *Where are you from?*
**A & B:** *We're from Asia.*
**Group:** *Are you Japanese / from Japan?*
**A & B:** *No, we aren't.*
**Group:** *Are you Chinese / from China?*
**A & B:** *Yes, we are!*

# I'm a journalist

## Listening

**1** 1.23 Listen to Tim and Kate. Write T (true) or F (false).

1 Tim and Anna are journalists. ___
2 Tim's married. ___
3 Kate's single. ___
4 Kate's famous. ___
5 Kate's a journalist. ___

**2** What's Tim's question to Kate? Listen again and check.

1 What's your job? 2 What's your work? 3 What do you do?

**3** 1.24 Match four of the photos with the dialogues. Listen and check. Practise the dialogues.

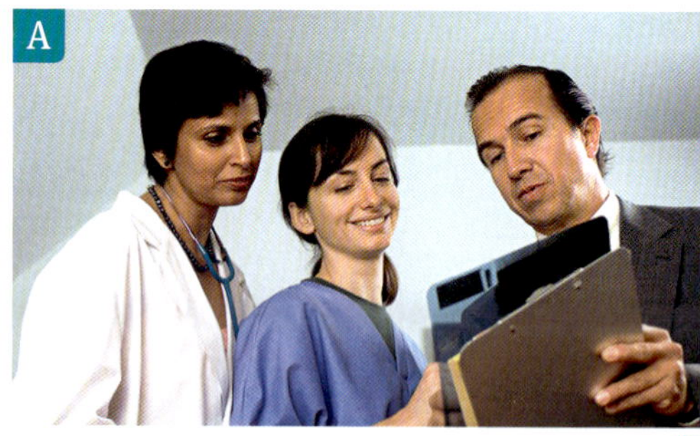

1 **A:** What do you do?
**B:** I'm a housewife.

2 **A** Are you doctors?
**B:** Yes, we are.

3 **A:** What do you do?
**B:** We're retired.

4 **A:** Are you a teacher?
**B:** No, I'm not. I'm an engineer.

**Tip**
**Special plurals**
housewife → house**wives**
waitress → waitress**es**

**4** 1.25 Name five more jobs. Word Bank 5, p. 68.

**5** In pairs, A choose a job from p. 68.
B ask about the job.

**B:** *What do you do?*
**A:** *I'm ... .*

**Tip**
Be careful!
✓ I'm a student.
✗ ~~I'm student.~~

## Grammar

**6** Guess your classmates' real jobs. Ask and answer.

**A:** *Are you a(n) ...?*
**B:** *Yes, ... . / No, ... .*
**A:** *What do you do?*
**B:** *I'm ... .*

**7** 1.26 Say 13–29 in English. Word Bank 1B, p. 64.

**Verb *be* + jobs**

| | nouns | adjectives |
|---|---|---|
| **singular** | I'm **a** journalist.<br>I'm not **a** chef.<br>Are you **an** actress? | I'm retired. |
| **plural** | We're journalist**s**.<br>They're engineer**s**.<br>Are you doctor**s**? | Are they unemployed? |

AB, p. 83. Ex. 1 ▶

## Reading

**8** 1.27 Listen and read the text. Match the underlined phrases and pictures 1–7.

1

2

3

4

### Different countries, different cultures

In the UK you can marry when you're 16. In France you can marry when you're 18. In parts of Russia you can marry when you're 14. In Iran a man can marry when he's 15 and a woman when she's 13.

In the UK you can drive a moped (50cc) when you're 16 and drive a car at 17. In Spain and Portugal you can drive a moped at 14 and a car at 17. And in New Zealand you can drive a car when you're 15!

In France you can buy cigarettes and buy alcohol when you're 16. In the USA you can buy cigarettes at 18 and alcohol when you're 21. In Brunei you can't buy alcohol but everybody can buy cigarettes.

And in Norway, you can work 12 hours a week when you're 13!

5

6

7

**Tip**

The verb *can* has one positive and one negative form.

| | | | |
|---|---|---|---|
| + | I/You/We/They | can | drive. |
| – | | can't | |

**9** Read the text again and complete the chart. Is your country the same or different?

| | (marry) | (drive a moped) | (drive a car) | (buy cigarettes) | (buy alcohol) | (work) |
|---|---|---|---|---|---|---|
| the UK | 16 | | | | | |
| parts of Russia | | | | | | |
| Iran | | | | | | |
| Spain & Portugal | | | | | | |
| New Zealand | | | | | | |
| France | | | | | | |
| the USA | | | | | | |
| Brunei | | | | | | |
| Norway | | | | | | |

**A:** *Italy is the same as the UK. You can marry when ... .*

**B:** *My country is different. You can't ... .*

# All about you

## Listening

**1** 1.28 What's your address? Word Bank 1C, p. 64.

**2** 1.29 Listen to Lars' phone message.

1 Who is the message for?

2 Complete the message:

Please c_ _ _ to m_ birthday p_ _ _ _ at e_ _ _ _ o'clock on F_ _day.

3 What's the name and address of the pub?

_ _ _phant's He_ _
_ _ _ Camden High Street
Camden

**3** Listen again and complete Lars' phone numbers.

Lars Solskjaer

02__________

79__________

**Tip**

**In phone numbers:**

0 = 'oh' or 'zero'   66 = double six

**In addresses:**

1546 = fifteen forty-six

**4** Ask your classmates for their addresses and phone numbers.

A: *What's your home address / work address?*

B: *(It's) ... .*

A: *What's your home number / work number / mobile number?*

B: *(It's) ... . / I don't have one.*

**5** 1.30 In pairs, say the names and addresses of the four restaurants on the web page. What types of restaurant are they? Listen and check.

http://www.foodlover.

In Camden in North London, these are the restaurants Food Lovers recommend:

The Great Wall
438 Victoria Avenue

Little Italy
409 Harley Street

Best Burgers
491 Cambridge Road

Super Sushi
489 Riley Street

**6** 1.31 Listen to Leo, Anna, Kate and Tim. Tick (✓) the correct sentence.

1 Leo's a waiter at a Chinese restaurant. ☐

2 Leo's the receptionist at his Japanese restaurant. ☐

3 Leo's the chef at his Italian restaurant. ☐

Which restaurant from Exercise 5 is Leo's?

**7** Listen again. Complete the information about Leo.

| | |
|---|---|
| Full name | Leo Jackson |
| Nationality | __________ |
| Occupation | __________ |
| Mobile number | __________ |
| Home address | 142, West Street |

**8** 1.32 Write the questions for the information in Exercise 7. Listen, check and repeat.

1 What's your full name?

2 What nationality ________ ________?

3 ________ ________ ________ ________?

4 ________ ________ ________ ________?

5 ________ ________ ________ ________?

## Writing

**9** Read this message to Foodlovers.com.
In pairs, complete and answer the questions.

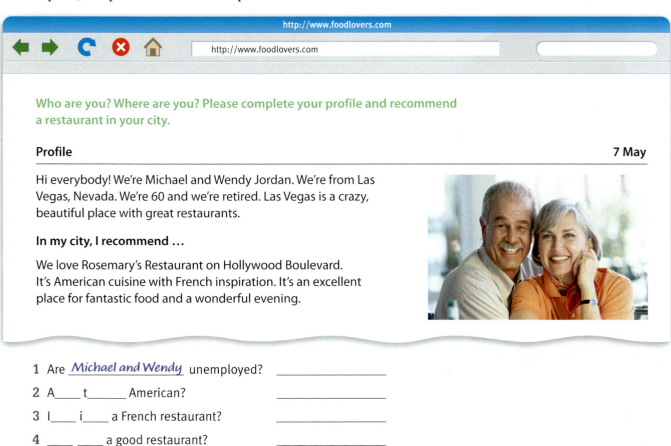

http://www.foodlovers.com

http://www.foodlovers.com

**Who are you? Where are you? Please complete your profile and recommend a restaurant in your city.**

**Profile** **7 May**

Hi everybody! We're Michael and Wendy Jordan. We're from Las Vegas, Nevada. We're 60 and we're retired. Las Vegas is a crazy, beautiful place with great restaurants.

**In my city, I recommend …**

We love Rosemary's Restaurant on Hollywood Boulevard. It's American cuisine with French inspiration. It's an excellent place for fantastic food and a wonderful evening.

1 Are *Michael and Wendy* unemployed? ________
2 A____ t_____ American? ________
3 I____ i____ a French restaurant? ________
4 ____ ____ a good restaurant? ________

**10** Read another message. Find and correct three mistakes in it.

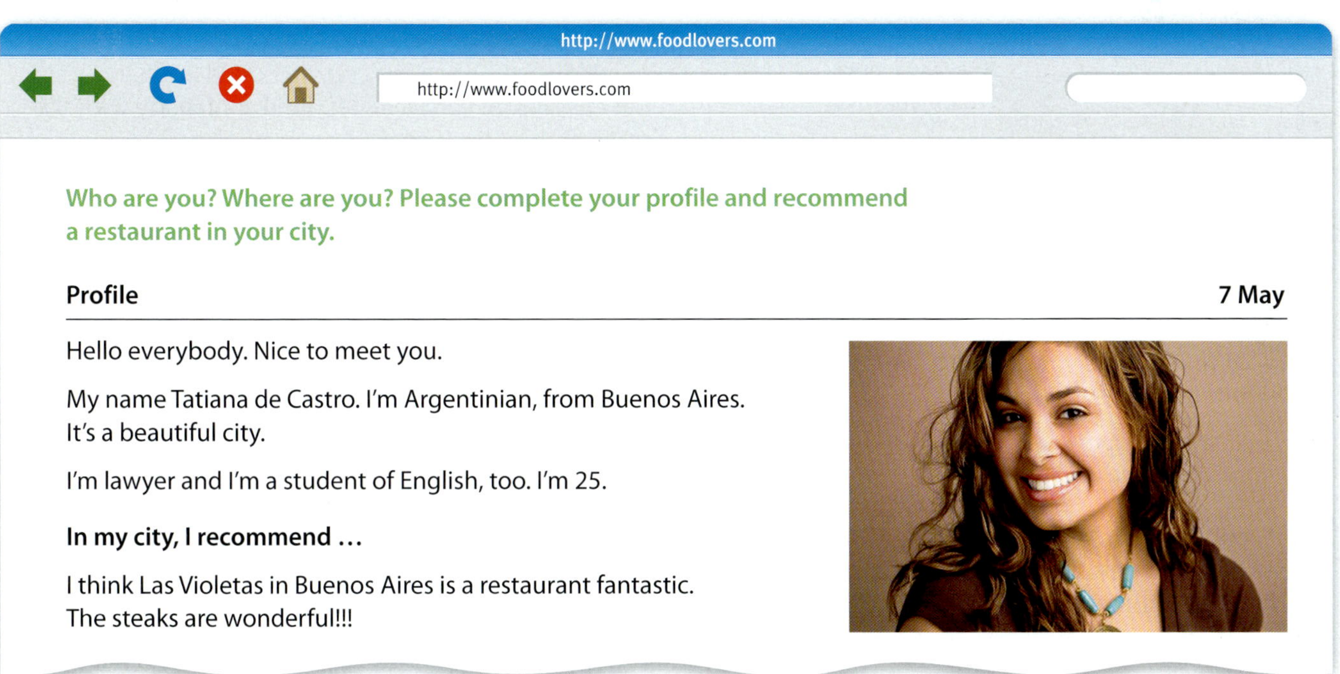
http://www.foodlovers.com

http://www.foodlovers.com

**Who are you? Where are you? Please complete your profile and recommend a restaurant in your city.**

**Profile** **7 May**

Hello everybody. Nice to meet you.

My name Tatiana de Castro. I'm Argentinian, from Buenos Aires. It's a beautiful city.

I'm lawyer and I'm a student of English, too. I'm 25.

**In my city, I recommend …**

I think Las Violetas in Buenos Aires is a restaurant fantastic. The steaks are wonderful!!!

**11** Write a message to Foodlovers.com. Write your profile and recommend a good restaurant in your city.

Go to Essential Grammar 1 p. 113

# 1 Revision

**1B 1** Play HELLO.
Get cards from your teacher.

A: *Good afternoon. Er ... Are you David Beckham?*

B: *No, I'm not.*
A: *Sorry!*
B: *It's OK. Goodbye.*

B: *Yes, I am.*
A: *Hello. I'm Tobey Maguire. Nice to meet you.*
B: *Nice to meet you, too.*

**1C 2** In pairs, test your memories. Walk round the class. How many things can you name in English in two minutes?

A: *This is a book, these are pens, that's a ... er ...*

B: *A door. That's a door. And this is a window. That's four.*

A: *OK, and these are keys. That's five. And ...*

**3** Test another pair. A from pair 1 ask A from pair 2. B from pair 1 ask B from pair 2. Which pair can remember more words?

A1: *What's this? / What are these?*

A2: *It's a(n) ... . / They're ... . I don't know. Is it a ...? Are they ...?*

A1: *Yes, it is. / Yes, they are. No, it isn't. / No, they aren't.*

**1D 4** 1.33 Complete the dialogue with the phrases in the box. Listen, check and repeat. Practise the dialogue in groups of three.

| I think | How are you | Nice to meet you, too |
|---|---|---|
| And you | No, I'm Canadian | This is my friend |

**Lucas:** Hey, Norma!

**Norma:** Hello, Lucas. (1) ______________________?

**Lucas:** Fine, thanks. (2) ______________________?

**Norma:** Fine, thanks, Lucas. (3) ____________________, Carol.

**Lucas:** Nice to meet you, Carol.

**Carol:** (4) ______________________.

**Lucas:** Are you American?

**Carol:** (5) ______________________. And you?

**Lucas:** I'm from Denmark.

**Carol:** Where in Denmark are you from?

**Lucas:** Copenhagen.

**Carol:** Oh, Copenhagen! (6) ______________________ Copenhagen's a fantastic city.

**Lucas:** Thank you!

**1E 5** In pairs, in two minutes, remember and write 15 jobs in English. Check your spelling on p. 68. Are they all correct?

**6** Play FIND YOUR INTERNATIONAL PARTNER.
Get cards from your teacher. Find somebody with the same nationality and job as you.

A: *Where are you from?*

B: *I'm German.*

A: *And what do you do?*

B: *I'm a footballer.*

A: *Good. I'm a German footballer, too.*

**1F 7** 1.34 Listen and tick (✓) the correct option.

**Teacher:** Please open your books at page ☐ 19 ☐ 90.

**Student:** Sorry, is it 19 or 90?

**Teacher:** It's ☐ 19 ☐ 90.

**Student:** Thank you.

**8** In pairs, practise the dialogue. Use numbers 13/30, 14/40, etc.

**9** Talk in pairs. Complete the questions then ask your partner.

| | you | your partner |
|---|---|---|
| Where ____ you from? | | |
| What nationality ____ you? | | |
| What ____ you do? | | |
| What ____ your mobile number? | | |
| ____ you married? | | |
| What's the ____ of your favourite restaurant ____ your city? | | |
| Who ____ your favourite actor or actress? | | |

**10** 1.35 Listen to Laura and Raphael's message to an online community. Write T (true), F (false) or ? (not in text).

1 Raphael's surname is Bernard. ___
2 They're French, from Lyon. ___
3 They're lawyers. ___
4 Lyon is an excellent city. ___
5 Laura and Raphael's work number is 3771-4563. ___
6 Laura's mobile number is 0771 49371. ___
7 Laura and Raphael's address is 1483 quai Charles-de-Gaulle. ___

**Unit 1 Song:** *Hello, Goodbye* The Beatles

To find the words, google lyric + the name of the song.

To find the video, google video + the name of the song and singer.

Make sure you use only legal websites!

Go to **Writing 1** p. 60 ▶

**11** Use the words in the box to complete the paragraph about Claire.

from think I'm but a

My name's Claire. (1)____________ (2)____________ secretary. I'm (3)____________ New York, (4) ____________ I live in Montreal. I (5)____________ Montreal is a fantastic city.

# In Paris on Thursday

## Speaking

**1** 2.1 Spell your surname in English. Word Bank 6A, p. 69.

**2** Say these acronyms. What other acronyms in English do you know?

| | | | |
|---|---|---|---|
| 1 | **CIA** | 5 | **MSN** |
| 2 | **DVD** | 6 | **CNN** |
| 3 | **FBI** | 7 | **UK** |
| 4 | **HBO** | 8 | **VIP** |

**3** Play HOW DO YOU SPELL ...? Use three words from Unit 1.

A: *How do you spell 'retired'?*

B: *I think it's R-E-T-I-R-E-D. Is that right?*

A: *Yes, you're right. / Sorry, you're wrong. It's ... .*

B: *OK. How do you spell ...?*

**4** 2.2 Look at the programme in Exercise 6. Listen and chant the days.

**5** Which two days rhyme? Which day has three syllables? (SYL-LA-BLES)

**Tip**

Use capital letters for days of the week.
**S**unday, **M**onday, etc.

## Listening

**6** 2.3 Listen to two Chinese tourists at the *Let's Go* travel agency. Complete their programme.

Let's Go
The best prices and the best service


**Tour programme for Mr & Mrs** (1) ___________

| | |
|---|---|
| Sunday | American Airlines flight (2) ___________ from New York JFK to Rome. |
| Monday | (3) ___________ |
| Tuesday<br>Wednesday | Spain |
| Thursday<br>Friday | (4) ___________ |
| Saturday | England<br>Evening: Delta Airlines flight (5) ___________ from London to New York. |

## Grammar

**Prepositions**

| | | |
|---|---|---|
| **on** | *days* | The flight is **on Sunday**. |
| **in** | *cities* | They're **in Boston** now. |
| | *countries* | Boston's **in the USA**. |

**7** Play MEMORY TEST.
**A:** Look at the programme in Exercise 6. Ask B questions.
**B:** Don't look at the programme. Answer A's questions. Look at the Grammar box for help with prepositions.

A: *Where are they on ...?* B: *They're in ... .*

A: *Are they in ... on ...?* B: *Yes, they are. / No, they aren't. They're in ... .*

AB, p. 86. Ex. 2 ▶

## Speaking

**8** Read about the Eurostar. Write (T) true or (F) false.

London to Paris in just
2 hours and 15 minutes.

**Eurostar** trains produce **ten times less $CO_2$** than planes.
Relax with phones, your laptop, drinks,
full restaurant service and no airport stress!

http://www.eurostar.com

1 Trains go from London to Paris in 145 minutes. ___

2 Planes produce the same $CO_2$ as trains. ___

3 You can use computers and buy food on the train. ___

**9** (2.4) Match the words and pictures. Listen, check and repeat. Which is your favourite?

1 _F_ beer
2 ___ coffee
3 ___ ice
4 ___ milk
5 ___ orange juice
6 ___ sugar
7 ___ tea
8 ___ mineral water
9 ___ wine

A B

**10** (2.5) Listen to Mr and Mrs Wang on the Eurostar. What do they drink?

Mr Wang ______________________

______________________

Mrs Wang ______________________

______________________

**11** Listen again and complete the dialogue.

 ?
**Attendant:** Would you like a (1) _drink_ ?

✓ 
**Mrs Wang:** Yes. (2) ____________, please.

?
**Attendant:** Milk?

✗
**Mrs Wang:** (3) ____________, thanks.

 ?
**Attendant:** Sugar?

✓
**Mrs Wang:** (4) ____________, please.

**Attendant:** Here (5) ____________ are, madam.

**Mrs Wang:** Thank (6) ____________.

**Attendant:** (7) ____________ welcome.

**Attendant:** And for (8) ____________, sir?

**Mr Wang:** Mineral (9) ____________ for me, please.

**Attendant:** (10) ____________?

✓
**Mr Wang:** Yes, (11) ____________.

**Attendant:** Here you (12) ____________.

**Mr Wang:** Thank (13) ____________ very much.

**12** Cover the dialogue in Exercise 11. Look at the icons and practise.

**13** In pairs, offer each other some drinks.

**A:** *Would you like a drink, madam / sir?*

**B:** *Yes, ... .*

# 2B How old is he?

## Reading

1 Say what you know about the people in the quiz photos.

A: *He's an actor.*

B: *She's American.*

### QUIZ: Know your celebrities! Who are these people?

A 
Shakira

B 
David Beckham

C 
Ewan McGregor

D 
Oprah Winfrey

E 
Bill Gates

F 
Salma Hayek

**1** ☐

She's from Mississippi, USA.

She's on TV a lot, but she isn't an actress now.

She's a TV presenter and writer. She's famous for her charity work.

She's about 55 years old.

**2** ☐

He's from Britain but he isn't English – he's Scottish.

He's a famous actor, and he's in many films, including *Moulin Rouge* and three *Star Wars* films.

He's about 40 years old.

**3** ☐

He's an American from Seattle.

He's very famous, but he isn't a film star.

He's the president of an important company.

He's about 55.

**4** ☐

She's from Medellín in Colombia, but she's fluent in Arabic, English, Italian, Portuguese and, of course, Spanish.

She's a famous singer and a very good dancer, too.

She's about 30.

**5** ☐

**6** ☐

2 Do the quiz. Match photos A–F with texts 1–4.

## Listening

3 2.6 Listen to Anna and Leo. Which two celebrities are they talking about? Tick (✓) the correct photos in the quiz.

4 Listen again and tick (✓) the questions you hear.

1 a ☐ How old is she?
b ☐ How old is he?

2 a ☐ Is she an actress?
b ☐ Is he an actor?

3 a ☐ Where's she from?
b ☐ Where's he from?

## Grammar

**5** Study the texts in Exercise 1 and questions in Exercise 4. Complete the Grammar box with *is*, *isn't* or *'s*.

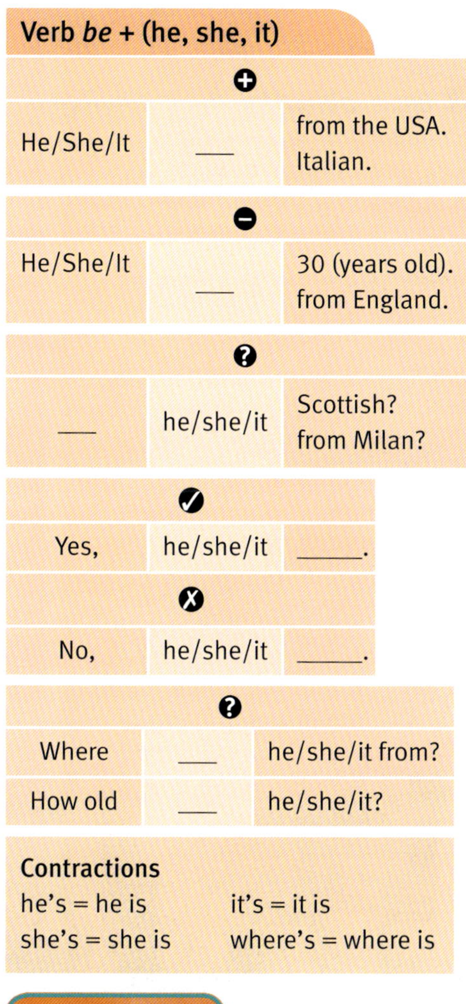

**Verb *be* + (he, she, it)**

| ⊕ | | |
|---|---|---|
| He/She/It | ___ | from the USA.<br>Italian. |

| ⊖ | | |
|---|---|---|
| He/She/It | ___ | 30 (years old).<br>from England. |

| ? | | |
|---|---|---|
| ___ | he/she/it | Scottish?<br>from Milan? |

| ✓ | | |
|---|---|---|
| Yes, | he/she/it | ____. |

| ✗ | | |
|---|---|---|
| No, | he/she/it | ____. |

| ? | | |
|---|---|---|
| Where | ___ | he/she/it from? |
| How old | ___ | he/she/it? |

**Contractions**

he's = he is　　it's = it is
she's = she is　　where's = where is

AB, p. 87. Ex. 2 ▶

## Pronunciation

**6** 2.7 Listen, repeat and link the words.

Is he ...　　Is she ...　　Is it ...

## Speaking

**7** Play TELEPATHY.

A: Turn to p. 68. Choose a job.
B: Guess who A is thinking about. How many guesses do you need?

**B:** *Is it a man or a woman?*
**A:** *A woman.*
**B:** *Is she a receptionist?*
**A:** *Yes, well done. / No, sorry, think again.*

**8** Look at Exercise 1 again. In pairs, talk about the other two celebrities in the quiz.

**9** Match sentences 1–6 and sentences a–f.

1 Kate Moss is a famous model. [e]
2 Angelina Jolie's American and about 35. [ ]
3 Damien Hirst's a famous British artist. [ ]
4 My new car's a red BMW. [ ]
5 Orhan Pamuk's a writer from Istanbul. [ ]
6 The Eiffel Tower's in Paris, France. [ ]

a He's about 55 and a Nobel Prize winner.
b It's about 120 years old.
c It's from the Leipzig factory in Germany.
d He's from Bristol in England and is about 45.
e She's about 35 and from South London.
f She's a beautiful ex-model and now a famous actress.

**10** In groups, talk about these people and things.

**A:** *Who's this? / What's this?*
**B:** *This is ... . He/She/It's a(an) ... . / I don't know!*
**A:** *Where's he/she/it from?*
**B:** *(I think) He/She/It's from ... . / I'm not sure.*
**A:** *How old is he/she/it?*
**B:** *(I think) He/She/It's (about) ... .*

# His music, her show, their charities

## Reading

**1** 2.8 Listen and read about Elton John and Oprah Winfrey. What are the names of their charities?

### Sir Elton John's millions for charity

Elton John is famous for his music, his glasses – and now his charity work! Elton's charity, the Elton John AIDS Foundation, raises millions of pounds for AIDS research.

### Oprah – not one charity, but three!

Oprah Winfrey's TV show has millions of fans. And Oprah Winfrey's three charities – The Oprah Winfrey Foundation, Oprah Winfrey's Angel Network and The Oprah Winfrey Operating Foundation – raise millions of dollars.

**2** Study the texts in Exercise 1. Match the phrases with *'s* and the correct meanings (1–4).

1 the charity of Elton John ________________

2 the money of Elton John ________________

3 the charities of Oprah Winfrey ________________

4 the TV programme of Oprah Winfrey ________________

AB, p. 88. Ex. 1 ▶

**3** In groups, connect the things in the photos with the celebrities in Lesson 2B. Use their names with *'s*, and the words in the photos A–I.

A: *I think photo A is Russell Crowe's oscar.*

B: *Yes, I agree. And I think photo F is … .*

C: *No, I think it's … .*

A
Oscar

B
charity

C
company

D
hometown

E
shirt

F
electric guitar

G
racing car

H
wife

I
twin sister and manager

**4** Read Kate and Leo's membership forms and sentences (1–9). Write *K* (Kate), *L* (Leo) or *F* (FFWC).

**Friends for the World's Children**
367 Market Street – Chichester – UK
Tel 1224 786 534 Fax 1224 786 538
info@ffwc.org

**Membership form**

| | |
|---|---|
| Name | Kate *Dixon* |
| Address | 229 West St<br>Camden<br>London |
| Home no. | 3725 6443 |
| Mobile no. | 8892 0255 |
| E-mail | kate.dixon@port.net |

**Friends for the World's Children**
367 Market Street – Chichester – UK
Tel 1224 786 534 Fax 1224 786 538
info@ffwc.org

**Membership form**

| | |
|---|---|
| Name | Leo *Jackson* |
| Address | 231 West St<br>Camden<br>London |
| Home no. | 3486 7721 |
| Mobile no. | 8777 4993 |
| E-mail | jaxon@yahoo.co.uk |

1 [F] Their address is 367 Market Street.
2 [ ] Her surname is Dixon.
3 [ ] His surname is Jackson.
4 [ ] Her address is 229 West Street.
5 [ ] His home number is 3486 7721.
6 [ ] Her mobile number is 8892 0255.
7 [ ] Their office is in Chichester.
8 [ ] His e-mail address is jaxon@yahoo.co.uk.
9 [ ] Their fax number is 1224 786 538.

**Tip**
info@richmond.com
at dot

## Grammar

**5** Complete the Grammar box with the words in the box.

her his my their your

**Singular possessives**

| | |
|---|---|
| I'm a TV journalist. | ____ home number is 9456723. |
| Do you have a mobile? | What's ____ phone number? |
| Elton's not here. | What's ____ contact number? |
| Oprah's a star. | What's ____ website address? |
| That's my cat. | What's **its** name? |
| **Plural** | |
| We're Russian. | **Our** hometown is St. Petersburg. |
| They're married. | What's ____ new address? |

AB, p. 88. Ex. 3 ▶

## Speaking

**6** 2.9 Listen. Who are these questions about? Write 1, 2 or 3.

Kate [ ] Leo [1] FFWC [ ]

**7** In pairs, ask and answer about Kate, Leo and FFWC. Use the information on the membership forms in Exercise 4. Count your partner's mistakes!

**A:** *What's Kate's surname?*

**B:** *It's Dixon. And what's her address?*

**8** Look at the picture from your teacher.

1 You have one minute to memorise the people and things in the picture.

2 In pairs, say if the things are next to the correct person.

**A:** *This is correct. It's his bag.*

**B:** *Yes, but these aren't his coins.*

**9** In pairs, ask questions to complete the profile.

**Profile of my partner**

First name ____________
Surname ____________
Mobile number ____________
E-mail address ____________
Hometown ____________
Favourite charity ____________
Favourite three possessions ____________
____________

**10** Change pairs. Ask about your new partner's old partner.

**A:** *What's his / her name?*

**B:** *It's ... .*

**A:** *And what's his / her ...?*

**B:** *... .*

**Tip**

He's my friend. ✓ His name is Leo.
✗ Your name is Leo.
She's my friend. ✓ Her name is Kate.
✗ Your name is Kate.

# 2D Do you have a big family?

## Listening

**1** 2.10 Who's your father's mother's grandchild? Word Bank 7, p. 70.

**2** 2.11 Look at the photo and listen to Tim and Kate. Number the names in the order Tim talks about them (1–6).

**Tip**
son(s) + daughter(s) = children (not sons)
father + mother = parents (not fathers)

| Order: | Inés ___ | Jane ___ | Jessica ___ | Mark ___ | Melanie ___ | Steve ___ |
|---|---|---|---|---|---|---|
| Photo: | ☐ | ☐ | ☐ | ☐ | ☐ | ☐ |
| | Job: ________ | Job: ________ | Age: ______ | Job: ________ | Age: ______ | Age: ______ |

**3** Listen again and match the people in the photo and names. Write A–F in the boxes.

**4** Listen again and write the correct jobs or ages. Which family member isn't in Australia now?

**5** 2.12 Circle the correct option. Listen and check.

1 **Kate:** *Are / Do* you have children?
**Tim:** Yes, I *am / do*. I have a son and two daughters.
**Kate:** Oh, really?

2 **Kate:** *Are / Do* you live alone?
**Tim:** No, I *'m / don't*. I live with my son.
**Kate:** How nice!

3 **Tim:** *Are / Do* you have a big family?
**Kate:** No, I *'m not / don't*. I only have my father and one sister.
**Tim:** Oh, I see ...

## Grammar

**6** Study the dialogues in Exercise 5 and complete the Grammar box.

**Present simple**

| ⊕ | | |
|---|---|---|
| I/You/We/They | ______ | two brothers. |
| | live | with a friend. |
| ⊖ | | |
| I/You/We/They | don't have | two brothers. |
| | ______ live | with a friend. |
| ? | | |
| ____ you/we/they | have | brothers and sisters? |
| | live | with a friend? |

| ✓/✗ | |
|---|---|
| Yes, I/you/we/they | do. |
| No, I/you/we/they | don't. |

**Contractions**
don't = do not

AB, p. 89. Ex. 2 ▶

## Pronunciation

**7** Listen again and repeat the dialogues in Exercise 5.

Link *do + you.*

Do you ...?

## Speaking

**8** Write four *Do you have ...?* questions to ask your partner. Guess the answers.
Then ask the questions. How many of your guesses are correct?

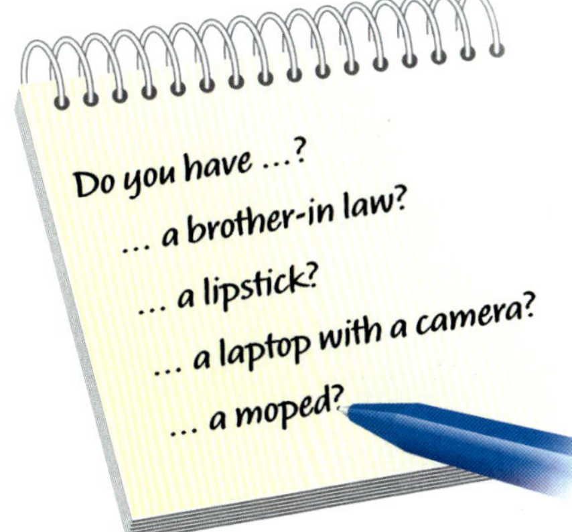

Do you have ...?
... a brother-in law?
... a lipstick?
... a laptop with a camera?
... a moped?


A: *Do you have a brother-in-law?*

B: *Yes, I do. I have three! / No, I don't. I'm not married and I'm an only child.*

**9** 2.13 Complete the questions. Listen and repeat.

**Our class!**

1. _____ you have children?
2. Do you have brothers _____ sisters?
3. Do you have _____ partner?
4. _____ you live alone?
5. Do you _____ in a flat or a house?
6. Do you live _____ a city, a town or a village?
7. _____ your grandparents dead or alive?
8. Do you have _____ big family?
9. How _____ nephews and nieces do you have?
10. Do you have _____ car or a motorbike?
11. _____ you think this is a good English book?
12. Do you _____ we have an excellent English teacher?

**10** Class survey. Choose three questions from Exercise 9 to ask every student in your class. Then stand up and ask your questions. Make a note of their answers.

## Writing

**11** Write a short report of your answers to show the class.

*My report*

*In this class, seven students live alone.*
*Nine students live with a partner.*
*Eleven students live in a flat and five live in a house.*
*One student lives with his twin brother.*
*No students live in a hotel or a caravan!*

# Meet your perfect partner

## Reading

**1** This is Tim's ex-wife, Jane. Read her message and complete her profile.

Perfect Partner.com

Welcome **JaneG** [logout]

HOME | MY ACCOUNT | MESSAGES | SEARCH | CHAT

**PROFILE**

Nickname: **JaneG**

I am: ☐ a man ☐ a woman

Born: 3 Jan

From: ______ Marital status: ______

I want to meet: ☐ a man ☐ a woman

Hi. I'm 32 years old. I'm divorced and I have three children. I'm English, but I live in Sydney now.

You, my perfect man, you're about 35 and you (1) work for a successful company. You (2) have a nice car and drive well.

You (3) speak Spanish very well, too – I love Spanish but I only speak a little! ¡*Hola guapo!* ¿*Cómo estás?* But, please, you (4) don't play football, OK? And you (5) don't smoke – it's a terrible habit.

Very important: you (6) like children a lot!

Do you want to meet me?

E-MAIL | INTERESTED? | PHOTOS

**2** Match the yellow phrases in Jane's message in Exercise 1 and pictures A–F. Write 1–6.

**3** 2.14 What does Jane's perfect partner say for each picture? Listen, check and repeat.

**A:** *I like children a lot.*

**B:** *I don't ... .*

**4** 2.15 What languages do you speak? Word Bank 4, p. 67.

## Listening

**5** (2.16) Jane's in a video-conference with W-guy, her first respondent. Listen to Part 1 of their dialogue and tick (✓) the correct option.

1 What's W-guy's real name?
☐ William ☐ Walter ☐ Wesley

2 How old is he?
☐ 24 ☐ 34 ☐ 39

**6** (2.17) Put Part 2 in order (1–6). Listen, check and repeat. In pairs, practise the dialogue.

[1] Do you have a car?
[ ] Yes, a little.
[ ] OK! What sports do you play?
[ ] Yes, I do. A Volvo.
[ ] Tennis and volleyball. I don't like football.
[5] Hmmm ... Do you smoke?

## Grammar

**Present simple – questions and answers**

| | | | | | | |
|---|---|---|---|---|---|---|
| Do | you we they | **have** a car? | ✓ | Yes, | you we they | **do.** |
| | | **smoke?** | | | | |
| | | **like** children? | ✗ | No, | | **don't.** |
| | | **play** football? | | | | |

| | | | | | |
|---|---|---|---|---|---|
| Where | **do** | you | **work?** | I | **work** for / in ... |
| What sports | | we | **play?** | We | **don't work.** |
| What languages | | they | **speak?** | They | **(don't) play ...** |
| | | | | | **(don't) speak ...** |

**7** (2.18) Study the Grammar box and complete Jane's questions. Listen and check. In pairs, practise the dialogue.

**Tip**
**Be careful!**
**A:** Do you like children?
**B:** ✓ Yes, I do.
✗ ~~Yes, I like.~~

**Jane:** ______________________________?
**W-guy:** I work for a small computer company.
**Jane:** Good. And ______________________?
**W-guy:** French and Spanish, but not very well.
**Jane:** ______________________________?
**W-guy:** Yes, I do. A lot!
**Jane:** Great!

**Tip**

I work | in a shop / an office / a bank. / for BMW / a big company.

AB, p. 90. Ex. 1 ▶

## Speaking

**8** Get cards from your teacher. Jane chats with two more respondents, PS35 and Bob-NY. In pairs, ask and answer their questions. Which respondent is perfect for Jane?

**9** In groups, ask and answer questions. How similar / different are you?

How old are you?
Where ... ?
What languages ... ?
What sports ... ?
I'm ... .
I work in ...
I speak ...
I play ...
Do you ...?
Yes, I do. / a lot. / a little. / very well.
No, I don't. / not very well.

# What do you do at the weekend?

## Speaking

**1** In groups, use the verbs and pictures to find three things you have in common.

**A:** *I have a dog. What about you? Do you have a pet?*

**B:** *Yes, I do. I have a dog, too. What about you?*

**C:** *I don't have a pet.*

**2** Jane and Larry meet face to face for the first time. Look at the photos. Where are they?

## Listening

**3** (2.19) Listen to the dialogue. Write T (true) or F (false).

1 Larry's car is a Mercedes. ___
2 His pet's name is Mercedes. ___
3 Larry's flat is small. ___
4 His office is in Bondi. ___
5 Larry's Australian. ___

**4** (2.20) Complete Jane's questions. Listen, check and repeat.

1 **Jane:** *Where* ______ live?
**Larry:** In a big flat in Bondi.

2 **Jane:** ______ work?
**Larry:** I work for Wilson & Johnson. It's a law office.

3 **Jane:** ______ that?
**Larry:** In the city centre, in Pitt Stret.

**5** In pairs, ask and answer the questions in Exercise 4. If you're a student or you don't work, talk about your school.

**A:** *Where do you study?*

**B:** *Here, at this school.*

**6** 2.21 Larry's talking about his free-time activities. Listen and match 1–5 and A–E.

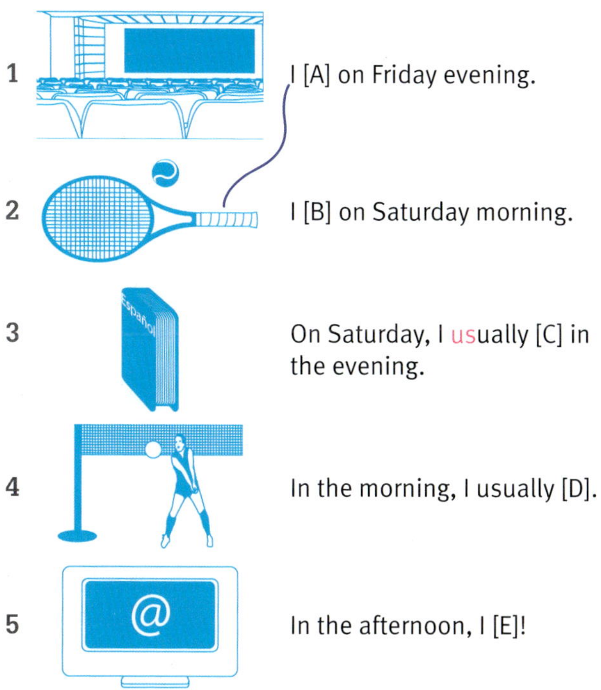

1 I [A] on Friday evening.

2 I [B] on Saturday morning.

3 On Saturday, I usually [C] in the evening.

4 In the morning, I usually [D].

5 In the afternoon, I [E]!

## Grammar

**7** Look at the expressions in Exercise 6 and complete the Grammar box with *in*, *on* or *at*.

**Prepositions: *in*, *on*, *at***

I (don't) usually work ...

| Part of the day | | Day | |
|---|---|---|---|
| _____ | the morning.<br>the afternoon.<br>the evening. | _____ | Monday.<br>Tuesdays. |
| | | **Day + part of the day** | |
| *at* | the weekend. | _____ | Friday morning.<br>Monday evenings. |

**8** 2.22 Do you go out a lot? Word Bank 8, p. 71.

**9** In pairs, compare your weekends. Are they similar?

**A:** *What do you do on Saturday morning?*

**B:** *I usually ... .*

## Reading

**10** 2.23 Lena Svensson has put a video on the Internet. Listen and read her videoscript.

*Hi! My name's Lena Svensson. I'm 32 years old. I'm single and I have two children, a boy and a girl. My son's name's Oskar. He's 10 years old. My daughter's eight. Her name's Emma. We live in a nice flat in Stockholm, near the Archipelago. We have a small dog.*

*I'm a freelance translator and I work at home here in the city, near the beach. I like it here. I speak English, German and Swedish very well and a little French, too. I study French at a big language school on Tuesdays and Thursdays.*

*At the weekend my children and I usually go to a sports club. I play volleyball or tennis and they play games with their friends. On Saturday evening I usually go out with friends or stay at home and watch TV. And on Sundays, I relax at home.*

*I don't smoke, and I don't like coffee or soft drinks. Just water!*

**11** Read the videoscript again and underline the information Lena and you have in common.

**12** Change the information that is different. Then write a videoscript about yourself.

Go to **Phrasebook 2** p. 77 ▶ Go to **Essential Grammar 2** p. 115 ▶

# 2 Revision

2A **1** Test your partner. Complete the sentences. Then spell the names and say the numbers for your partner to write.

1 My favourite name for a man is ___________ and for a woman is ___________.

2 My car / moped / motorbike number is ___________________.

**2** Choose and spell five words from Word Banks 1–5 for your partner to write.

**3** 2.24 Put the dialogue in the correct order (1–9). Listen, check and repeat. Then practise with a partner, using other drinks.

- [ ] Sugar?
- [ ] Here you are.
- [3] Milk?
- [ ] You're welcome.
- [ ] Good evening. Would you like a drink, madam?
- [ ] Thank you.
- [ ] Yes, tea, please.
- [ ] Yes, please.
- [6] No, thanks.

2B **4** 2.25 Read and complete the dialogue with *is he*, *'s he*, *he isn't* or *he's*. Listen, check and repeat. Practise with your partner.

**Ricky:** Hmm. This pasta is great! Oh, excuse me a moment. Hello?

**Manal:** Oh, mobile phones! So, Bea, where are you from?

**Bea:** I'm American, from Boston. And you?

**Manal:** Oh, I'm Egyptian, from Cairo.

**Bea:** And Ricky? Where (1)_________ from?

**Manal:** Guess!

**Bea:** Oh, I don't know. (2)_________ Canadian?

**Manal:** No, (3)_________.

**Bea:** Is he from Britain?

**Manal:** Yes, he is. (4)_________ from Manchester, England.

**Bea:** And how old (5)_________?

**Manal:** I think (6)_________ about 30. And yes, (7)_________ single! Very single!

**Bea:** Hmmm. I see.

**5** Complete the dialogues. Practise them.

1 **A:** Where _____ Kate _________?
**B:** _________________ from the USA.

2 **A:** _________________ Leo from?
**B:** _________________ from Britain.

3 **A:** Where _____ you and your family from?
**B:** _________________________________

**6** Play MAN, WOMAN OR THING? Get cards from your teacher.

**A:** *A man, a woman or a thing?*

**B:** … .

**A:** *Is he/she/it a/an actress / singer / monument / film, etc.?*

**B:** *Yes, … . / No, … .*

**A:** *Is he/she/it from …?*

**B:** *Yes, … . / No, … .*

**A:** *Is she/he/it … years old?*

**B:** *Yes, … . / No, … .*

**A:** *Is he/she/it …?*

**7** Celebrities. How old are they?

**A:** *How old is Tom Cruise?*

**B:** *I don't know … Well, I think he's about 45 years old.*

2C **8** Match the famous people with their original names.

| | |
|---|---|
| 1 Woody Allen's original full name | a Coppola |
| 2 Jennifer Aniston's original surname | b Thomas Cruise Mapother IV |
| 3 Tom Cruise's full name | c Maurice Micklewhite |
| 4 Michael Caine's real name | d Anastassakis |
| 5 Nicholas Cage's original surname | e Alicia Foster |
| 6 Jodie Foster's original name | f Allan Stewart Konigsberg |

**Unit 2 Song:** *Wonderful World*, Sam Cooke

To find the words, google lyric + the name of the song.

To find the video, google video + the name of the song and singer.

**9** 2.26 Complete the text with *your*, *his*, *her* or *their*. Listen and check.

These are very famous people. (1)______ name's Angelina Jolie and (2)______ name's Brad Pitt. (3)______ children are from different countries (Cambodia, Ethiopia, Namibia and Vietnam). (4)______ names are Maddox (a Welsh surname), Zahara, Shiloh, Pax, Knox and Vivienne. They're a very different but beautiful family.

What's (5)______ opinion of Brad and Angelina and (6)______ family?

Post your answer at www.brangelina&kids.com

**10** 2.27 Replace words in italics with *his*, *her* or *their*. Listen and check.

**Meet Bart Simpson**

*His*
~~Bart's~~ name's Bart and he has a sister. *Bart's sister's* name's Lisa. *Bart and Lisa's* mother and father are Homer and Marge Simpson. Bart has a baby sister, too. *Bart's* baby sister, Maggie, is just one year old. *Bart's* address is 742 Evergreen Terrace, Springfield. Bart and Lisa have a cat and a dog. *Bart and Lisa's* cat's name is 'Snowball 2' and *Bart and Lisa's* dog's name is 'Santa's Little Helper'.

2D **11** Answer the questions.

1 Who's your father's father? My ____________.

2 Who's your sister's brother's mother's husband? My ____________.

3 Who's your brother-in-law's wife? My ____________.

4 Who's your grand-daughter's father's mother? My ____________.

Go to Writing 2 p. 61 ▶

**12** In pairs, guess your partner's possessions.

1 A: Guess for Box 1. Tick, cross or change the number.
B: Guess for Box 2. Tick, cross or change the number.

2 A: Tell your partner what you think.
B: Listen and tell your partner how many guesses are correct.

**A:** *I think you have a big car, you don't have an old bike, and you have two MP3 players.*

**B:** *Three correct guesses. My turn.*

3 Correct your partner's wrong guesses.

**B:** *I have a small car, not a big car. I only have one MP3 player, ... .*

| 1 | 2 |
|---|---|
| a big car | a small house |
| an old bike | a big flat |
| an MP3 player | a Japanese TV |
| a dictionary | a new mobile |
| a digital camera | a ten euro note |
| two computers | a guitar |

2E **13** Tick (✓) the activities you do. Then, in pairs, ask and answer the questions. Find three things you have in common.

| | Me | My partner |
|---|---|---|
| drink coffee with sugar | | |
| play golf | | |
| drive well | | |
| smoke | | |
| study English on Saturdays | | |
| work on Sundays | | |

**A:** *Do you smoke?*

**B:** *No, I don't.* OR *Yes, I do. / Yes, a little. / Yes, a lot.*

**14** 2.28 How do you pronounce the vowels in these words? Word Bank 6B, p. 69.

English fantastic hotdog more
full run verb mineral water

2F **15** Tell your partner about your 'best friend'. Include name / age / marital status / where from / job.

*Her name is Maria. She's thirty years old and she's single. She's from Budapest and she's a civil servant.*

# Let's watch a DVD tonight

## Listening

**1** 3.1 Look at the picture and listen. Who's the phone call for?

**2** Listen again. Put the words in order.

1 phone Tim you answer please the can?
2 hello course of yes.
3 please I to speak can Anna?
4 sure please moment just a
5 you Anna for it's.

**Requests**

| | | ⊕ | | |
|---|---|---|---|---|
| Can | you<br>I | answer the phone,<br>speak to Mr Grant, | please? | Sure.<br>(Yes,) of course.<br>OK.<br>No problem. |

## Grammar

**3** 3.2 Study the requests in the Grammar box. Complete pictures 1–4. Listen, check and repeat.

1 A: _________ have a glass of water, please?
B: Yes, of course. Here you are.

2 A: _________ open the window, please?
B: Sorry, no. Not just now. I'm cold.

3 A: Excuse me. _________ lend me your pen?
B: OK, sure.

4 A: _________ use your mobile, please? It's an emergency.
B: No problem. Here you are.

**4** In pairs, ask and answer.

| A: Can | I<br>you | lend me<br>have<br>open<br>close<br>use | your<br>the<br>a(n) |  | please? |
|---|---|---|---|---|---|



B: Sure. Here you are. / Sorry, no. Not just now.

## Listening

**5** 3.3 Listen and answer these questions.

1 What are Leo's two suggestions?
2 Which suggestion does Anna say yes to?
3 What time?

**6** Read and complete the dialogue with the words in the box. Listen again and check. Practise the dialogue in pairs.

a can't come drink it's go see you

| | |
|---|---|
| **Anna:** | Anna Costa. |
| **Leo:** | Hi, Anna. (1)________ Leo. |
| **Anna:** | Oh, hello, Leo! |
| **Leo:** | Listen, let's go out tonight. Let's (2)________ to (3)________ club. |
| **Anna:** | I'm sorry, Leo. I (4)________. I'm really tired today. |
| **Leo:** | Well, let's have a (5)________, then. (6)________ to my restaurant! |
| **Anna:** | Oh, er ... OK, why not? |
| **Leo:** | Is seven o'clock good for (7)________? |
| **Anna:** | Perfect! |
| **Leo:** | Right, then. See you later. |
| **Anna:** | (8)________ you at seven. Bye. |

## Grammar

**7** Complete the suggestions in the Grammar box.

**Suggestions**

| | + | − |
|---|---|---|
| Let's (1)_____ out tonight.<br>(2)_____ go (3)_____ a club.<br>Let's (4)_____ a DVD. | Sure.<br>That's (5)_____ good idea.<br>OK, (6)_____ not? | Sorry, (7)_____ can't. |

AB, p. 93. Ex. 2 ▶

## Speaking

**8** In pairs, use the verb phrases in Word Bank 8, p. 71 to make suggestions.

A: *Let's go for a walk.*

B: *Sorry, ...*

**9** 3.4 Play ARE YOU (HUNGRY)? Word Bank 9, p. 72.
A: Choose an adjective.
B: Guess how A feels.

B: *Are you (hungry)?*

A: *No, I'm not. Try again. / Yes, I am. My turn. Ready? Are you ...?*

How many guesses do you need?

**10** 3.5 Put the dialogue in the correct order (1–8). Listen, check and repeat.

- [ ] Hey, Rita. It's Lars.
- [ ] 1 Hello. Can I speak to Rita, please?
- [ ] That's a great idea!
- [ ] Hi, Lars.
- [ ] Listen, I'm really bored. Let's go out.
- [ ] Rita here.
- [ ] OK. Let's go shopping.

**11** In pairs, phone your partner. Make suggestions, say 'Yes' or make excuses. Use adjectives and verbs from Word Banks 7 and 8.

A: *Can I speak to ..., please?*

B: *... here.*

A: *... .*

# 3B Ordinary people?

## Reading

**1** 3.6 Listen and read Biography 1. Who is it?

**Biography 1**

This 'ordinary' man lives in New York and goes to Columbia University. He's an excellent scientist and studies Physics. He also works as a photographer for the *Daily Bugle* newspaper. He has a wife, Mary Jane Watson, a model and actress, but he doesn't have children.

After contact with a radioactive spider, he gets superpowers. When he changes into a superhero he's really strong. He can't fly but he can jump very high and he can run up walls. He's very, very fast and he uses a fantastic liquid to stop bad people. He isn't very big. He has a special red and blue suit. He doesn't wear glasses. The actor Tobey Maguire plays this superhero in the Hollywood films. His name is ...?

**2** In groups, listen and read the text again. Stop after each sentence with underlined words. Communicate the meaning of the 13 underlined nouns, adjectives or verbs. Mime, draw or give examples.

A: *Scientist – for example, Albert Einstein ... .*

B: *Yes, yes, I understand. It's the same in my language.*

C: *And, Physics is, er, a subject from school. Like, um, Maths.*

D: *That's right. Or Chemistry. Physics is very difficult for me ... .*

## Grammar

**3** Study the verbs in yellow in Exercise 1 and complete the Grammar box.

**Present simple (he, she)**

| | + | | − |
|---|---|---|---|
| He<br>She | lives in New York.<br>g___s to Columbia University.<br>st____s Physics.<br>ch_____s into Spiderman.<br>u__s a fantastic liquid.<br>h__ a red and blue suit. | He<br>She | **doesn't live** in Washington.<br>________ **go** to school.<br>________ **fly**.<br>_____ ______ glasses.<br>**doesn't** ______ children. |

have + s = **has** /hæz/
go + s = **goes** /gəʊz/

**Contractions**
doesn't = does not

AB, p. 94. Ex. 1 ▶

## Pronunciation

**4** 3.7 The usual pronunciation of *-s* endings is /z/ or /s/. Listen and repeat the six positive sentences in the Grammar box. Which two verbs have an extra syllable for the *-s* ending?

**5** 3.8 In pairs, read and complete the verbs in Biography 2. Who is it? Listen and check. Who's your favourite superhero?

**Biography 2**

She (1) live__ in Africa and she (2) work__ as a teacher. Her real name's Ororo Munroe. She's beautiful! She (3) ha__ long white hair and (4) d_____n't wear glasses.

But she isn't ordinary! When she (5) change__ into a superhero, she (6) wear__ a special black suit. She (7) ha__ extraordinary superpowers. She (8) fl___ very fast and she can see at night. She (9) use__ the weather, the sea and the stars to stop bad people. She's one of the X-Men and the actress Halle Berry (10) play__ her in the X-Men films. Professor X, the leader of the X-Men (11) give__ her a new, superhero name. This name is ...

## Speaking

**6** Do the quiz. Circle the correct facts, 1–18. Compare with a partner.

**A:** *I think a typical British person has a car.*

**B:** *I agree. / No, I think he or she doesn't have a car.*

**7** 3.9 Listen and check your answers. Give yourself one point for each correct answer. What's your total?

**8** In pairs, cover the quiz and look only at the pictures. Can you remember and say the 18 correct sentences?

**9** Write five sentences about a 'typical' man or woman from your country.

1 *A typical Spanish woman has a car.*

2 *She drives very fast.*

**10** In groups, read and compare your ideas. Do you agree?

# ORDINARY PEOPLE?!

**How much do you know about the British?
What do you think a typical British person does, likes, thinks, plays and talks about?
Where does he or she live and go?**

A typical British person …

1 has / doesn't have a car.

2 drives / doesn't drive very <u>fast</u>.

3 smokes / doesn't smoke.

4 drinks tea and beer / coffee and wine.

5 has / doesn't have a pet.

6 has one child / about 1.8 children.

7 likes / doesn't like the Queen.

8 goes / doesn't go to the pub at weekends.

9 lives in a house / flat.

10 wears / doesn't wear a suit.

11 goes for a walk / goes for a run for exercise.

12 plays football / tennis.

13 reads / doesn't read a newspaper.

14 speaks two languages / only speaks English.

15 goes / doesn't go to university.

16 watches / doesn't watch TV in the evenings.

17 talks about the weather / football.

18 flies to Spain / the USA for a holiday.

**Total: /18**

# Does he like you? Yes, he does!

## Speaking

**1** Look at the picture and words. In pairs, say what you remember about this man.

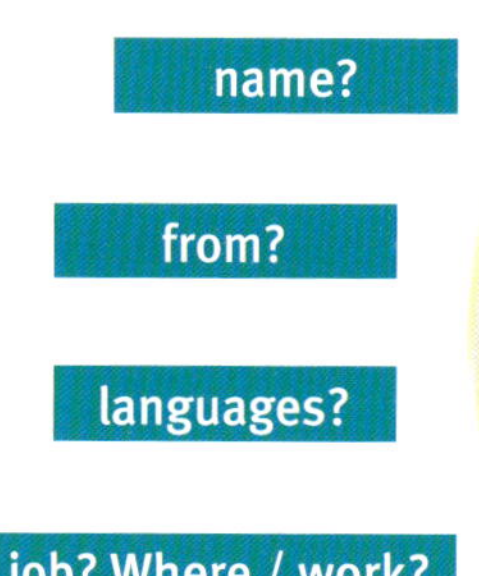


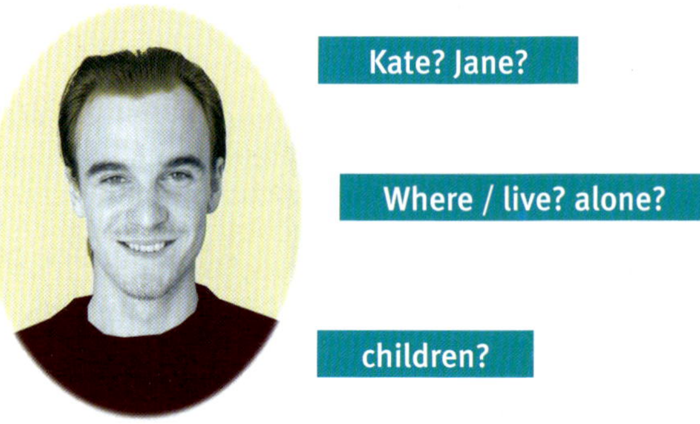


## Listening

**2** 3.10 Kate and Polly are friends from school. Read their chat and match Polly's questions (1–8) with Kate's answers. Listen and check. Did you remember all this information about Tim?

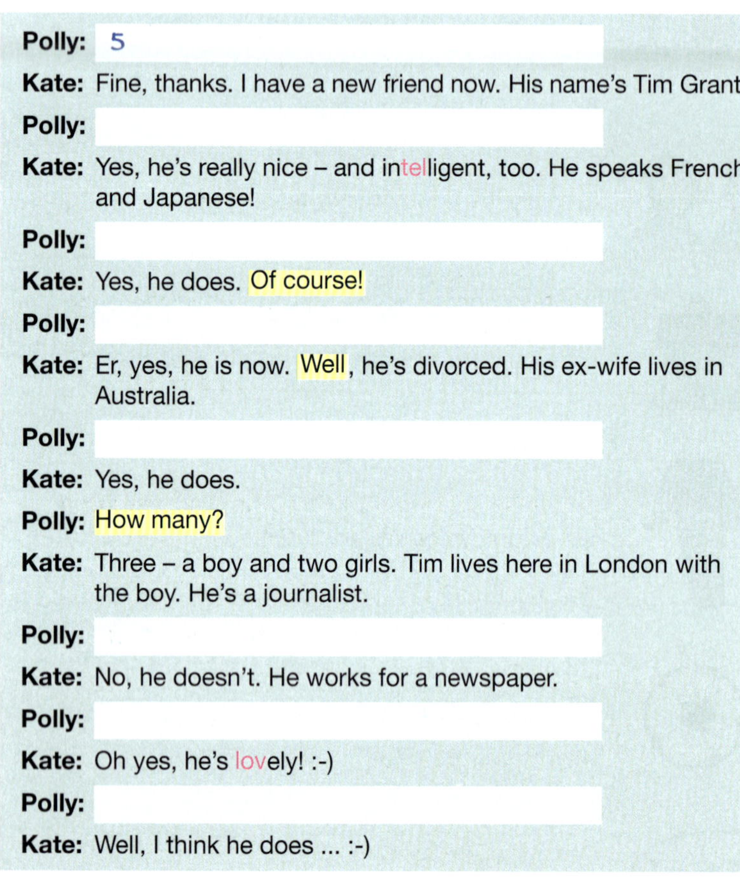

**Polly:** 5
**Kate:** Fine, thanks. I have a new friend now. His name's Tim Grant.
**Polly:**
**Kate:** Yes, he's really nice – and intelligent, too. He speaks French and Japanese!
**Polly:**
**Kate:** Yes, he does. Of course!
**Polly:**
**Kate:** Er, yes, he is now. Well, he's divorced. His ex-wife lives in Australia.
**Polly:**
**Kate:** Yes, he does.
**Polly:** How many?
**Kate:** Three – a boy and two girls. Tim lives here in London with the boy. He's a journalist.
**Polly:**
**Kate:** No, he doesn't. He works for a newspaper.
**Polly:**
**Kate:** Oh yes, he's lovely! :-)
**Polly:**
**Kate:** Well, I think he does ... :-)

1 A journalist? Really? Does he work on TV?
2 Does he speak English, too? :-)
3 Does he have children?
4 Great! Is he nice? :-)
5 So, how are you?
6 An important question: does he like you?
7 :-) Is he single?
8 I see ... And is he ... nice?

How do you say the expressions in yellow in your language?

## Grammar

**3** Look at Polly's questions 1, 2, 3 and 6 and Kate's answers. Complete the Grammar box.

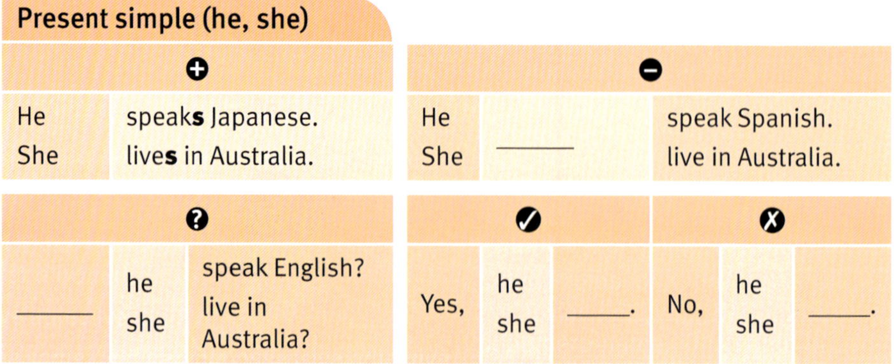

**Present simple (he, she)**

| + | | − | | |
|---|---|---|---|---|
| He<br>She | speak**s** Japanese.<br>live**s** in Australia. | He<br>She | ______ | speak Spanish.<br>live in Australia. |

| ? | | | ✓ | | | ✗ | | |
|---|---|---|---|---|---|---|---|---|
| ______ | he<br>she | speak English?<br>live in Australia? | Yes, | he<br>she | ______. | No, | he<br>she | ______. |

## Pronunciation

**4** 3.11 Complete dialogues 1–4. Listen and repeat. How do you pronounce:

1 Does he/she in the questions?
2 does/doesn't in the answers?

1 **Kate:** Tim's a journalist.
**Polly:** Really? ______________ work on TV?
**Kate:** No, ______________.

2 **Kate:** Tim works a lot.
**Polly:** I see. ______________ work on Sundays?
**Kate:** Yes, ______________.

3 **Kate:** My friend Anna's from Italy.
**Polly:** Oh! ______________ speak English well?
**Kate:** Yes, ______________.

4 **Kate:** And Anna has a new car!
**Polly:** Great! ______________ drive very fast?
**Kate:** No, ______________.

AB, p. 95. Ex. 1 ▶

## Speaking

**5** Look at the photos and answer the questions.

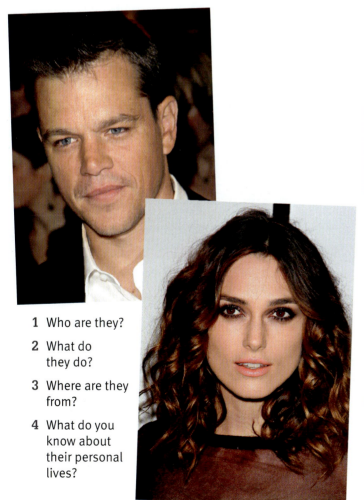

1 Who are they?
2 What do they do?
3 Where are they from?
4 What do you know about their personal lives?

**6** Get a card from your teacher. Read the information about one of the actors. Complete the chart with ✓ (Yes), ✗ (No) or ? (I don't know).

| | Matt | Keira |
|---|---|---|
| work in soap operas | ✗ | |
| do a lot of exercise | | |
| eat meat | | |
| smoke | | |
| sing or dance well | | |
| support a sports team | | |
| play a musical instrument | | |
| have children | | |
| have a pet | | |

**7** The same or different? In pairs, find five differences between Matt and Keira.

**A:** *Does Matt do a lot of exercise?*

**B:** *Yes, he does.*

**A:** *Keira does a lot of exercise, too. So that's the same.*

OR

**A:** *Keira doesn't do a lot of exercise. So that's one difference.*

## Writing

**8** Write five sentences about someone you know well. Use the phrases in the box.

like (animals) | support a team | live alone
speak English | play (football / the piano)
have a car / bike | eat / drink a lot | smoke
cook / dance well | do a lot of exercise
stay in / go out a lot | read / use a computer a lot

**The father in my host family.**
*He doesn't like dogs.*
*He has a small car.*
*He ... .*

**9** In pairs, ask and answer about the person in Exercise 8.

**A:** *Who's the person?*

**B:** *The father in my host family.*

**A:** *Does he like dogs?*

**B:** *Yes, he ... . / Yes, I think so.*

**A:** *Really? Does he ...?*

**B:** *No, he doesn't. / I don't know. / I don't think so.*

# Look at the time!

## Listening

**1** (3.12) Listen to Tim and Anna at work. Look at the TV guide.

1 Complete the speech bubbles with *late* and *tired*.

2 Circle Anna's favourite TV programme on the TV guide.

3 What type of programme is it?

4 Why does Anna say she likes this programme?

***Your* UK TV Guide**

**Terrestial TV Listings on 9th August 2008**

Saturday : Sunday : Monday: Tuesday : Wednesday : **Thursday** :

| BBC 1 | | BBC 2 | |
|---|---|---|---|
| **17.00** | MI High | **11.00** | Danger Mouse: The Trip to America (More...) |
| **17.25** | Newsround (More...) | **11.10** | Top Cat: Farewell, Mr Dibble (More...) |
| **17.35** | Neighbours (More...) | **11.35** | The Munsters (More...) |
| **18.00** | BBC News (More...) | **12.00** | Film: The Hawaiians (1970) (More...) |
| **18.30** | BBC London News (More...) | **14.10** | Hands On Nature: Estuaries (More...) |
| **19.00** | The One Show (More...) | **14.45** | Escape to the Country (More...) |
| **19.30** | EastEnders (More...) | **15.45** | Flog It! Exeter (More... |
| **20.00** | The Inspector Lynley Mysteries: Limbo (More...) | **16.30** | Ready Steady Cook (More...) |
| **21.30** | Traffic Cops: Pushing Their Luck (More...) | **17.15** | The Weakest Link |
| **22.00** | BBC Ten O'Clock News (More...) | | |

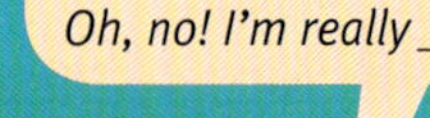


*I'm really _______!*

**2** What time is it? Complete the answers for each time.

8.00 It's ______ o'clock.

7.30 It's seven __________ . = It's half past ______.

5.15 It's ______ fifteen. = It's quarter past ______.

14.50 It's two __________ . = It's ten to ______.

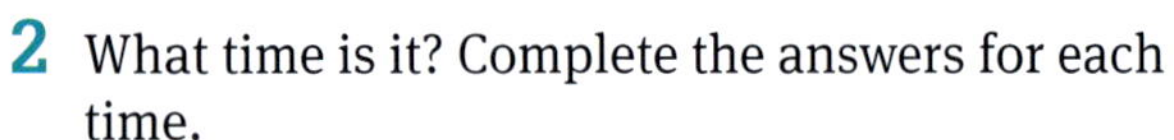

**3** (3.13) Listen to Tim and Anna. Tick (✓) the correct option.

1 What time is it?

a ☐ 6.40 b ☐ 7.20 c ☐ 7.30

2 What time does her programme start?

a ☐ 7.35 b ☐ 7.30 c ☐ 7.45

**4** (3.14) What's the time? Word Bank 10, p. 73.

## Speaking

**5** Play RACE THE CLOCK!
A: Say all the times on the TV guide in one minute to your partner. Swap roles.
B: Say all the times in one minute. Use the other 'system'.

**A:** *Five o'clock, five twenty-five … .*

**B:** *Five o'clock, twenty-five past five … .*

## Pronunciation

**6** Listen to your teacher. Repeat and link the words.

What time is it? It's one o'clock.

**7** Play BIG BEN.
Get cards from your teacher.

**A:** *What time is it?*

**B:** *It's twenty to eight.*

**A:** *You mean it's seven forty?*

**B:** *Yes, that's right!*

## Listening

**8** 3.15 Listen to Tim and Vicki. Complete the TV Guide.

## Grammar

**9** Look at the Grammar box and complete sentences 1–4 with *at*, *at about* or *on*.

| | | |
|---|---|---|
| What channel<br>When | | is it on? |
| What time does it | | start?<br>end? |
| It | 's on | Friday. |
| | | MTV. |
| | starts **at** 6.15 p.m. | |
| | ends **at about** 7.30. | |

1 We use ________ for exact times.

2 We use ________ for days and channels.

3 We use ________ for an approximate time.

4 We can say 'on on' too! For example,
Question: When's it ____?
Answer: It's on ____ Tuesdays ____ 5 p.m.

AB, p. 96. Ex. 3

## Speaking

**10** In groups, find common favourite programmes.

**A:** *What's your favourite TV programme?*

**B:** … .

**C:** *What channel is it on?*

**B:** *(It's on) on … .*

**D:** *When is it on?*

**B:** *(It's on) on … .*

**A:** *What time does it start / end?*

**B:** *(It starts / ends) at (about) … .*

# What time do you get up?

## Speaking

**1**  What do you do every day? Word Bank 11, p. 74.

**2** Ask your classmates questions 1–8 below. Find a different person for each activity and write their names.

A: *Do you ...?*

B: *Yes, ... . / No, ... .*

**Tip**

before ← ● → after — A is before B. 11 is after 10.

| | Names |
|---|---|
| 1 get up before 6.30 a.m. | |
| 2 listen to the radio in the morning | |
| 3 have a shower before breakfast | |
| 4 start work or school after 9.00 a.m. | |
| 5 have a big lunch | |
| 6 get home before 7.00 p.m. | |
| 7 study another language | |
| 8 do their homework | |

**3** In groups, compare your findings.

A: *Lars gets up before 6.00 a.m.*

B: *Rita doesn't have a big lunch.*

## Reading

**4** 3.17 Listen and read the film review. Answer questions 1–4.

1 What and who is the review about?

2 What type of man is he? Find two negative adjectives and one positive adjective in the review.

3 Are his books, the film and his life all romantic?

4 Do you know the film? Would you like to see it (again)?

In the romantic comedy, *As Good as It Gets*, Melvin Udall (Jack Nicholson) is a horrible man. He's a successful writer of romantic stories, but he has no love in his life and he doesn't have any family or friends.

He does exactly the same things every day. He has breakfast in the same restaurant at the same table at the same time and with the same waitress, Carol (Helen Hunt), every day. For breakfast, he always eats sausages, bacon and eggs and drinks coffee. He doesn't work in an office. He writes at his computer at home from Monday to Friday. He works a lot!

At weekends, Melvin stays at home. He reads a lot, plays the piano and doesn't have a social life. Melvin is a difficult man but, before the film ends, he changes. He helps Carol, she starts to like him and ... ❤❤❤

An excellent film. Don't miss it. ★★★★★

## Grammar

| **Present simple (he, she)** <br> ***Wh-* questions and answers** | | | |
|---|---|---|---|
| What time | does | he <br> she | start work? |
| What | | | do in the morning? |
| Where | | | work? |

| | |
|---|---|
| He <br> She | starts work at seven a.m. |
| | goes to school in the morning. |
| | works in the theatre. |

**5** Look at the Grammar box and complete the questions about the review.
In pairs, ask and answer the questions.

1 What ________ ________ do?
2 Who ________ ________ hate?
3 Where ________ ________ ________ breakfast?
4 What does ________ have ________ breakfast?
5 When ________ ________ work?
6 Where ________ ________ work?
7 What instrument ________ he ________?
8 ________ ________ ________ do at the weekend?

AB, p. 97. Ex. 2 ▶

## Speaking

**6** Get a card from your teacher. Get more information about Melvin. Read the information and complete half the text.

**Here's a typical day in Melvin's life:**

He gets up at (1)______ a.m. and has a shower. At about (2)______ a.m. he goes to the same restaurant and has breakfast. He finishes at exactly (3)______. He starts work at (4)______ p.m. and finishes at about (5)______. At (6)______ p.m. he has dinner and at exactly (7)______ p.m. he watches the TV news. He goes to bed at (8)______.

**7** In pairs, ask and answer questions to complete the text.

**A:** *What time does Melvin ...?*

**B:** *At (about) ... .*

**8** In pairs, look again at p. 74. Use the pictures to ask and answer about your typical day.

**A:** *What time / When / What do you usually ...?*

**B:** *At (about) ... .*

**9** Tell the class about your partner. Are you (very) similar or (really) different?

**A:** *I think Nina's very different / similar to me. She ... .*

**10** Talk in groups.
A: Think about a person you know well. Say if it's a man or a woman.
Group: Ask for information about A's person. Guess who it is.

**A:** *My person is a man / woman.*

*What does he / she ...?*
*What time does he / she ...?*
*Where does he / she ...?*
*Is he / she your ...?*
*Does he / she ...?*

# He always leaves home early

## Listening

**1** 3.18 Listen to Kate and Anna on the phone. Tick (✓) the correct option.

1 ☐ Kate phones Anna.
☐ Anna phones Kate.

2 Kate suggests they have dinner
☐ at Leo's restaurant.
☐ at Gordon Ramsay's restaurant.

3 Kate asks Anna to
☐ make a reservation.
☐ phone Leo.

4 They agree to meet at
☐ quarter past eight.
☐ quarter to eight.

## Speaking

**2** In groups, suggest what to do after class. Use Word Bank 8, p. 71 for ideas.

A: *Let's ... .*

B: *That's a good idea.*

C: *OK. What time?*

**3** 3.19 Kate, Tim, Anna and Leo are at the restaurant. Read the dialogue and circle the correct option. Listen and check.

| | |
|---|---|
| **Kate:** | Hey! Great food, isn't it? |
| **Anna:** | Delicious! And I'm really (1) *hungry / bored!* |
| **Tim:** | Yes, (2) *a / the* meat's excellent. So, do you guys watch a lot of food programmes (3) *in / on* TV? |
| **Leo:** | Yes, I do. I love Gordon Ramsay. I'm (4) *your / his* number one fan! My favourite programme (5) *is / are* 'Kitchen Nightmares'. Do you know it? |
| **Anna:** | No, what channel is it (6) *on / in*? And when? |
| **Leo:** | (7) *At / On* Thursday evening, (8) *at / on* More 4. |
| **Tim:** | What time does it (9) *start / starts*? |
| **Leo:** | At nine p.m. |
| **Kate:** | (10) *Is / Does* it really good, then? |
| **Leo:** | Oh, it's wonderful! I'm a very (11) *busy / tired* man, but I never miss it! |

**4** Do you watch a lot of TV? In pairs, ask and answer. Do you watch similar programmes?

A: Do you watch a lot of TV ...?

B: Yes, I do. / No, I don't. What about you?

A: I watch a little / a lot. / No, I don't like TV.

B: Do you watch ...

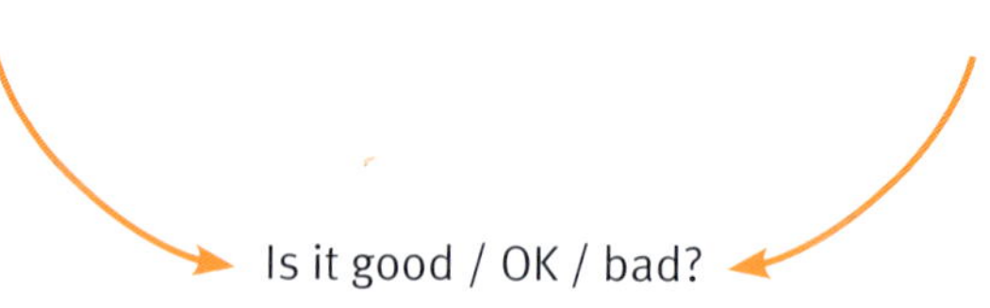

A: Yes, I do. It's great. Do you watch it, too?

B: Yes, I do. I love it. / No, I don't.

A: No, I don't. What channel ...?

When ...? / What time ...?

Is it good / OK / bad?

## Pronunciation

**5** 3.20 Make eight complete questions about Gordon Ramsay. Listen, check and repeat. Stress the underlined words.

1 how many restaurants / have?
*How many restaurants does he have?*

2 what time / leave home?

3 what time / get home?

4 where / come from?

5 where / live?

6 how many children / have?

7 what sports / play / weekends?

8 what type / shows / make?

## Reading

**6** Read Gordon Ramsay's biography in one minute. Cover the text. In pairs, answer the questions in Exercise 5. Can you remember all the answers?

A: *How many restaurants does he have?*

B: *A lot – I don't remember the number.*

**A: *I remember. He has ... .***

# Gordon Ramsay – a *very* busy man

Gordon Ramsay's a famous chef. He has a lot of restaurants – eight in London, two in the USA and one in Japan! He writes, too and has eight different cookbooks now. He always leaves home at 7.30 a.m. to go to work and he doesn't usually get home before 1.00 a.m. He doesn't have a lot of free time.

He comes from Scotland, but he lives with his wife Tana and four children in a big house in South London. He usually spends weekends at home when he can and never misses a chance to play football. He plays really, really well.

Ramsay's a famous 'TV chef', too. He makes reality shows like *Kitchen Nightmares* and *The F Word* and they're always very successful. If you like food and cooking, don't miss them!

## Grammar

**7** Read about Leo. How do you say the yellow words in your language?

**Adverbs of frequency**

Leo Jackson's **always** busy.

He's a chef, and he has a restaurant in Camden.

He always leaves home very early.

He **usually** works late.

He doesn't usually work on Sundays.

He **sometimes** plays tennis at weekends.

He **never** misses a chance to play tennis.

Circle the correct option, *before* or *after*.

*Always, usually, sometimes, never* go:

1 *before / after* the verb *be*.

2 *before / after* other verbs.

## Speaking

**8** Compare Leo and Gordon Ramsay. Look at the example. Find four more things that they have in common.

A: *Leo's a chef with a restaurant in London and Gordon's a chef with restaurants in London, too.*

B: *That's one thing they have in common. We need four more things.*

**9** In pairs, use *always*, *usually*, *sometimes* or *never* to talk about these activities. Find three things you have in common. Then tell the class.

1 work (late on Fridays)
2 play (football at the weekend)
3 stay at home (in the evening)
4 go shopping (on Saturdays)
5 watch (soap operas)
6 have a big (lunch)

A: *I sometimes work late on Fridays. What about you?*

B: *I never work late on Fridays! I always go home early.*

**10** In pairs, talk about a 'busy' person you know. Ask and answer about:

- name / nationality / age / family / occupation
- daily routine: morning / afternoon / evening
- weekends

Go to **Phrasebook 3** p. 78 ▶ Go to **Essential Grammar 3** p. 117 ▶

# 3 Revision

3A **1** Complete the sentences. Are they requests (R) or suggestions (S)?

1 Let's have a party _on_ Saturday. [S]
2 Can I have ______ cappuccino, please? [ ]
3 Can you open ______ windows, please? [ ]
4 ______ watch a DVD later. [ ]
5 Can I speak ______ Tricia, please? [ ]
6 ______ you meet me this afternoon? [ ]

**2** 3.21 Complete the dialogue with two requests and one suggestion from Exercise 1. Listen and check. In pairs, practise it. Change the names and times.

**Mac:** Can (1)______ ______ ______ Tricia, ______?
**Tricia:** This is Tricia.
**Mac:** Hello, Tricia. It's Mac.
**Tricia:** Oh, hi, Mac!
**Mac:** Listen. (2)______ ______ meet me this ______?
**Tricia:** Sure, I can. Come to my house. Is five o'clock good for you?
**Mac:** It's perfect! Thank you very much. Hey, listen. (3)______ watch ______ ______ later. What about *Mission Impossible 3*?
**Tricia:** Oh, er ... OK, why not?
**Mac:** Right, then. See you later.
**Tricia:** See you. Bye.

3B **3** 3.22 Pronunciation. Listen and write 1, 2 or 3. Listen again and repeat.

1 = /z/ 2 = /s/ 3 = /ɪz/

a Jack watches a lot of TV. [3]
b He reads a lot of magazines, too. [ ]
c He likes Spider-Man. [ ]
d Spider-Man wears a special suit. [ ]
e Peter Parker relaxes at weekends. [ ]
f Storm works as a teacher. [ ]
g Batman has a fantastic car. [ ]
h Jack's dog runs very fast. [ ]
i Jack's cat drinks a lot of milk. [ ]

**4** Play WHO IS IT?
Get cards from your teacher. Talk about the people on the cards.

**5** Match the verbs (1–8) and phrases (a–h). In pairs, tell your partner three true sentences about you and three true sentences about a person you know.

| | |
|---|---|
| 1 do | a a party |
| 2 go | b exercise at the gym |
| 3 stay | c to music |
| 4 have | d time online |
| 5 listen | e video games |
| 6 play | f TV or DVDs |
| 7 spend | g at home |
| 8 watch | h out with friends |

A: *I go out with friends on Saturdays.*
B: *My sister spends time online in the evenings.*

3C **6** Complete the dialogues. Practise in pairs.

1 A: My friend Julia's an actress.
B: Really? _Does she_ work in films?
A: Yes, she does. She works on TV, too.

2 A: My car's very old. It doesn't go very fast.
B: __________ have a CD player?
A: No, it doesn't. I think I need a new car!

3 A: Paolo's in Germany.
B: Great! __________ speak German?
A: No, he doesn't. But he speaks a little English.

4 A: My sister's in Japan.
B: Great! ____________ speak Japanese?
A: Yes, very well. Her partner is from Tokyo.

**7** Get cards from your teacher. In pairs, find out more about Tim.

A: *Does Tim / he ...?* B: *Yes, he does. / No, he doesn't.*

**8** 3.23 How do you pronounce the vowels in these words? Word Bank 6C, p. 69.

now pair we're coins tourist

**9** 3.24 Can you remember the names of ten places in a town? Word Bank 12, p.75.

an airport

**Unit 3 Song:** *Girls just wanna have fun*, Cyndi Lauper

To find the words, google lyric + the name of the song.

To find the video, google video + the name of the song and singer.

**9** In pairs, ask and answer questions with the phrases in the box. Remember three interesting things about your partner to tell the class.

**Your computer habits!**

have a laptop have wifi
like computers use computers a lot
spend a lot of time online chat
watch music videos make CDs
call people on Skype go to Internet cafés
buy things online play games
read the news watch DVDs
have a favourite website?

**A:** *Do you chat on the Internet?*

**B:** *Yes, a lot. / Yes, a little. / No, I don't.*

**A:** *Who with?*

3D **10** Put the words in order. In pairs, talk about your favourite radio station and programmes.

1 radio programme / what's / favourite / your
What's ____________________?

2 is / station / on / what / it
____________________?

3 on / when / it / is
____________________?

4 does / time / start / what / it
____________________?

5 end / what / it / does / time
____________________?

**A:** *What's your favourite radio programme?*

**B:** *It's ... .*

3E **11** Circle the correct option. In pairs, practise the dialogue. Change Livia's words to make them true for you.

**Roger:** What do you usually do (1) *in / on* Mondays?

**Livia:** Well, I get up (2) *from / at* about seven o'clock and go to work.

**Roger:** What time do you start work?

**Livia:** I work (3) *from / before* 8.30 (4) *after / to* 5.30.

**Roger:** Do you usually have lunch?

**Livia:** Yes, I have lunch (5) *from / before* 1.00 until 2.00 p.m.

**Roger:** And what time do you get home?

**Livia:** I usually go out with some friends (6) *after / before* work, so I'm home (7) *from / at* about eight.

Go to Writing 3 p. 62 ▶

**12** In groups of three, imagine a typical day in Sarah's life. Use Word Bank 11 to make sentences about her day.

Sarah's a student. She doesn't have a lot of money and the rent for her flat is very high. So she works a lot and her life is very busy.


*On Mondays Sarah gets up at five o'clock in the morning.*

3F **13** Make six true sentences about you. Use the words in 1–6 and *always*, *usually*, *sometimes* or *never*. Use different days and times, too. Then compare in pairs.

*I never have lunch at home from Monday to Friday.*

1 I have lunch at home

2 I do exercise

3 With my friends I talk about

4 I use a computer

5 I drive

6 I ____________________

**14** In pairs, look at Word Bank 8. Use the pictures to compare your weekends. Find five interesting differences to tell the class.

**A:** *I usually go for a run on Sundays.*

**B:** *Really? I never go for a run.*

# Have a good trip!

## Reading

**1** 4.1 What are your favourite places? Word Bank 12, p. 75.

**2** 4.2 Listen and read about Edinburgh. Write T (true) or F (false). Would you like to go there?

1 Edinburgh is the capital of Scotland. ___
2 For tourists, it has a lot of old and new attractions. ___
3 The Edinburgh Arts festival is in August for two weeks. ___
4 It takes six hours to travel from London to Edinburgh. ___

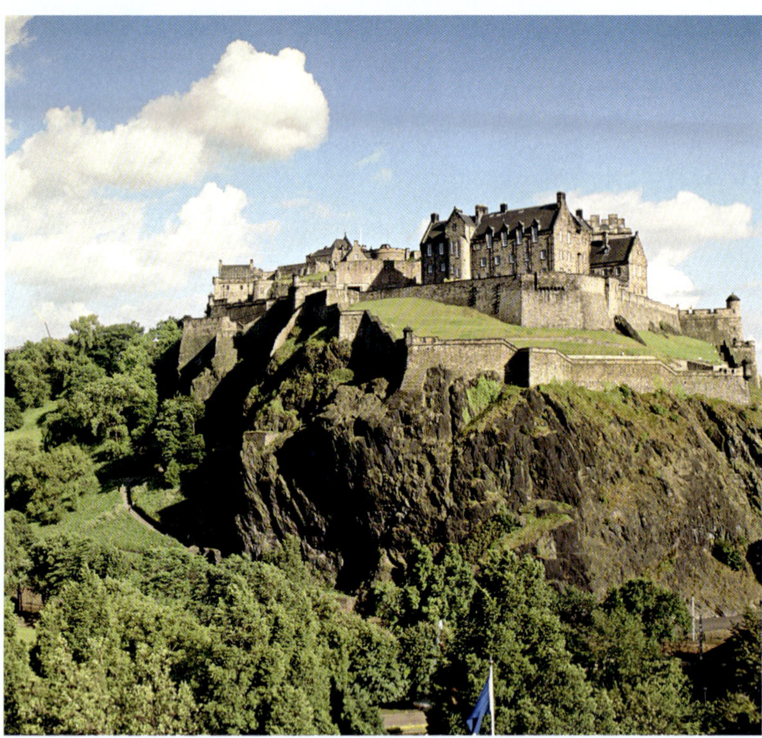

Welcome to Edinburgh, population 450,000 and Scotland's beautiful capital city since 1437. Edinburgh has a lovely castle, a fantastic palace and many other important monuments.

It's an exciting modern city, too, with excellent museums and art galleries, great cafés, pubs and all types of restaurants and nightclubs.

Edinburgh has a lot of art and music festivals, too. The famous Edinburgh Festival starts on the second Sunday in August and finishes three weeks later. It's Europe's number one Arts festival.

Fast trains from all London stations to Edinburgh take about five hours. A flight from Heathrow, Gatwick, London City or Stansted airports takes about one hour and 20 minutes.

Visit www.edinburgh.org or www.visitscotland.com

## Listening

**3** 4.3 Lars has a class project about Edinburgh. He phones Tourist Information. Listen and complete the times.

For information about tourist attractions, go to:

Edinburgh & Scotland Tourist Information Centre
3 Princes Street
Edinburgh, Scotland EH2 2PQ

**Opening and closing times**

| | |
|---|---|
| Monday – ________ | 9.00 a.m. – _____ p.m. |
| ________ – Saturday | _____ a.m. – ________ |
| Sunday | _______ – ________ |

**4** 4.4 Now Lars tries the Information Centre in London. Listen and complete the times on the brochure.

**Some opening and closing hours in Edinburgh (April to October)**

| Services | Open | Close | Days |
|---|---|---|---|
| Main Shopping Centres | 11.00 a.m. | 5.00 p.m. | Sun |
| | (1) ________ | 6.00 p.m. | Mon–Wed / Sat |
| | 10.00 a.m. | (2) ________ | Thu – Fri |
| The Post Office | 9.00 a.m. | (3) ________ | Mon – Fri |
| | 9.00 a.m. | (4) ________ | Sat |

## Grammar

**5** (4.5) Study the Grammar box and complete the questions. Listen, check and repeat.

1 What time ________ the shopping centres open on Sundays?

2 What time ________ the post office close on Saturdays?

**_What time?_ + Present simple (it, they)**

| | | | | | | |
|---|---|---|---|---|---|---|
| What time | does | it | open?<br>close?<br>leave?<br>arrive? | It | opens<br>closes<br>leaves<br>arrives | at ... . |
| | do | they | | They | open<br>close<br>leave<br>arrive | |

AB, p. 100. Ex. 1 ▶

**6** Get a card from your teacher. In pairs, talk about other opening and closing hours in Edinburgh.

**A:** *What time does / do ... open / close on ...?*

**B:** *It opens / closes / They open / close at ... .*

## Speaking

**7** In groups, talk about the opening hours in your country. Are they similar to Scotland?

banks museums nightclubs the post office restaurants
shopping centres shops the main tourist attractions

**A:** *What time ... open / close? Do banks open on Sunday in ...?*

**B:** *I'm not sure. / I have no idea.*

**8** (4.6) Lars decides to go to Edinburgh for the weekend. He's now at Kings Cross station, London. Listen and complete the ticket.

Single / return
Next train leaves: ________ arrives: ________
Price: £________

**9** Listen again and order the dialogue 1–13. Listen, check and repeat.

☐ **Man:** Would you like a single or a return?
6 **Lars:** Here you are.
☐ **Man:** It leaves at 9 a.m. from platform 7.
☐ **Lars:** Return, please. How much is it?
1 **Man:** Can I help you?
☐ **Lars:** Thank you very much.
11 **Man:** At 2.15 p.m.
☐ **Lars:** Yes, can I have a ticket to Edinburgh, please?
☐ **Man:** Thank you. Here's your ticket.
☐ **Lars:** And what time does it arrive?
☐ **Man:** £62.
8 **Lars:** What time does the next train leave, please?
☐ **Man:** Have a good trip!

**10** Get a card from your teacher. In pairs, buy train tickets.

# When's your birthday?

## Reading

**1** Get a card from your teacher. Read about one of the music festivals. Tick (✓) the types of music they play. Use the words in the box.

| | | |
|---|---|---|
| ☐ opera | ☐ country | ☐ pop |
| ☐ heavy metal | | ☐ jazz |
| ☐ classical | ☐ rock | |

MUSIC IN THE SUMMER
Edinburgh International Festival
Salzburg Festival
Montreal International Jazz Festival

**2** In groups, talk about the festivals.

1 Ask and answer about each.
- a Where is it?
- b How old is it?
- c How long is it (how many days / weeks)?
- d What type of music do they play?

2 Look at the three cards together.
- a Find the names of two months. ________ and ________ .
- b Find three dates. *10th August* , ________ and ________ .
- c Which festival does the photo on the card show?

## Pronunciation

**3** 4.7 Listen and write the months in the correct word stress box.

| | | |
|---|---|---|
| ~~January~~ | February | ~~March~~ |
| April | May | June |
| July | August | ~~September~~ |
| October | November | December |

| The months | | | | |
|---|---|---|---|---|
| Ooo | O | Oo | oO | oOo |
| *January* | *March* | ________ | ________ | *September* |
| ________ | ________ | ________ | | ________ |
| | ________ | | | ________ |
| | | | | ________ |

## Grammar

**4** 4.8 How do you say the dates in Exercise 2? Complete the ordinal numbers. Listen, check and repeat.

**Ordinal numbers**

| | | | |
|---|---|---|---|
| 1st | first | 11th | eleven___ |
| 2nd | second | 12th | twelf___ |
| 3rd | third | 13th | ________th |
| 4th | fourth | | |
| 5th | fifth | 20th | twentieth |
| 6th | _____th | 21st | twenty-_______ |
| 7th | ________th | 22nd | twenty-_______ |
| 8th | eighth | 23rd | __________-third |
| 9th | nin___ | | |
| 10th | _____th | 30th | ______________ |
| | | 31st | ______________ |

*What's the date today?*

*I think it's the ...*

**Tip**

We write: 7th September
7 September

We say: (It's ) **the** seventh **of** September.

## Pronunciation

**5** 4.9 Listen and repeat. Be careful with 'th'.

1 Fifth Avenue and Fourth Street

2 20th Century Fox

3 thirteen months

4 1303 and 1333

5 Thirty-three thousand people think Thursday is their thirtieth birthday.

What other English words do you know with the *th* spelling?

**6** Look at the Grammar box and complete the sentences.

**Dates**

| | |
|---|---|
| | When's US Independence Day? |
| Months | It's **in** July. |
| Dates | It's **on** 4th July. |
| | When's your birthday? |
| Days | It's **on** Sunday! |

1 New Year's Eve is ______ 31st December.

2 Thanksgiving Day in the USA is ______ the fourth Thursday ______ November.

AB, p. 101. Ex. 2 ▶

## Speaking

**7** Get a card from your teacher. When's Independence Day? Ask and answer.

A: *When's Independence Day in Argentina?*

B: *It's on 9th July. When's Independence Day in Brazil?*

**8** When are the festivals and celebrations in your country? Are they public holidays?

*In Britain, Valentine's Day is on 14th February. But it isn't a public holiday.*

**9** 4.10 Emma works with Anna and Tim. Listen to Emma and Anna and tick (✓) the correct option.

1 When's Tim's birthday?

☐ On Friday ☐ In October ☐ On 4th September

2 What type of music does Tim like?

☐ Rock ☐ Jazz ☐ Opera

**10** When are *your* birthdays? Stand up and ask your class. Organise yourselves into a line across the class from birthdays in January to birthdays in December.

A: *When's your birthday?*

B: *(It's) On ... . / In ... .*

A: *OK. So you're before me. My birthday's on ... .*

**11** Before you sit down, tell the class your birthdays. Which is a) the most common month for birthdays and b) the most common date for birthdays?

*We have four birthdays in March and three birthdays on the 23rd!*

# Musicals? I'm sorry, I really hate them

## Listening

**1** 4.11 Kate's at Tim's birthday party. Listen to extracts from the dialogue. Tick (✓) Kate's favourite types of films and music.

**Films**

☐ action ☐ cartoons ☐ comedies ☐ dramas ☐ musicals ☐ science fiction ☐ thrillers ☐ westerns

**Music**

☐ classical ☐ country ☐ disco ☐ reggae ☐ jazz ☐ opera ☐ rock ☐ techno

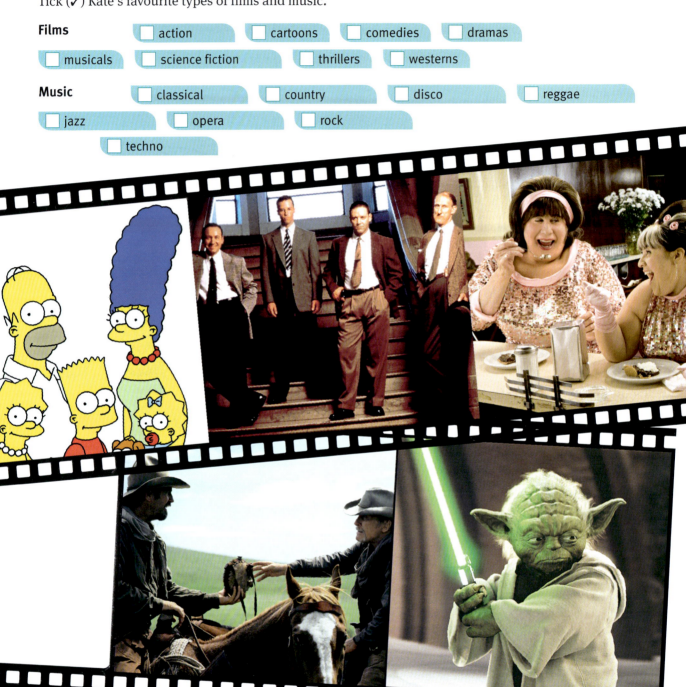

**2** Circle two types of film and two types of music that you usually like in Exercise 1. Put a cross (✗) next to one type of film and one type of music that you don't usually like. Find someone in class who's the same as you.

**A:** *What types of film do / don't you usually like?*

**B:** *I like thrillers. LA Confidential is my favourite film.*

**3** 4.12 Kate's talking to Tim at the party. Listen and number the adjectives in the order you hear them (1–8).

☐ boring ☐ excellent ☐ fabulous ☐ good ☐ great ☐ horrible ☐ interesting ☐ wonderful

**4** Read and complete the dialogue with *do*, *of*, *for* or *is*.

| | |
|---|---|
| **Tim:** | So, Kate, (1)______ you like this song? |
| **Kate:** | Oh, that's Justin Timberlake. He's very good. |
| **Tim:** | Yes, I like him a lot! How about Bono? I think he's fabulous. (2)______ you like him, too? |
| **Kate:** | Oh yes. Justin and Bono are great. I love them! |
| **Tim:** | Your favourite type (3)______ music (4)______ rock, then. |
| **Kate:** | Yes, I like it very much. And country, too. They're my favourite. |
| **Tim:** | And (5)______ you like the cinema? |
| **Kate:** | Yes! My favourite actress (6)______ Kate Winslet. What (7)______ you think (8)______ her? |
| **Tim:** | Oh, she's exciting. I like her, too. And what type (9)______ films (10)______ you like? |
| **Kate:** | Thrillers, musicals ... But not science fiction films. I don't like them. They're horrible! |
| **Tim:** | Come on, Kate. Science fiction (11)______ wonderful! (12)______ example, the *Matrix* films are very interesting. Now, musicals?! I'm sorry, I really hate them. They're boring! |
| **Kate:** | Boring? No way. What about *Dreamgirls*, (13)______ example, or *Hairspray* or *Chicago* or *Grease* ...? |

## Grammar

**5** Read the dialogue in Exercise 4 again. Draw lines to make true sentences.

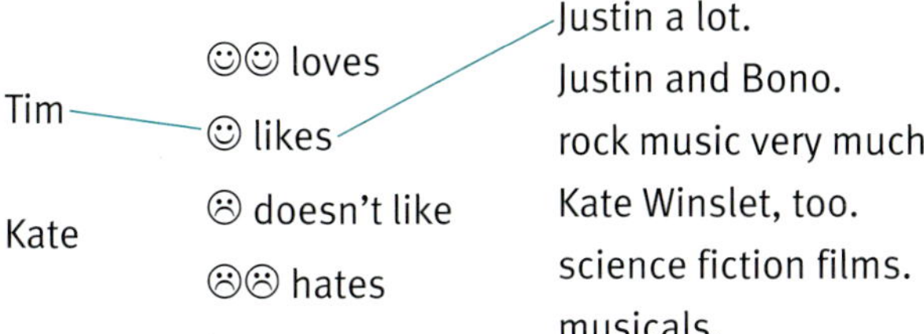


**6** Study the dialogue in Exercise 4 again. Complete the Grammar box with the pronouns in yellow.

**Object pronouns**

| Subject | Object |
|---|---|
| I | me |
| you | you |
| he | ______ |
| she | ______ |
| it | ______ |
| we | us |
| they | ______ |

AB, p. 102. Ex. 2 ▶

## Pronunciation

**7** 4.13 Listen and circle the stressed word in each sentence. Listen again and repeat.

1 I love you.
2 She hates us.
3 Do you like her?
4 I don't like it.
5 We like them.
6 Do you love me?

## Speaking

**8** Get a card from your teacher. In pairs, talk about Kate and Tim. Are they very similar?

**A:** *What does Kate / Tim think of ...?*
**B:** *He / She ... .*

**9** What do you think? Write two names for each category. In groups, ask and answer.

| | | |
|---|---|---|
| film: | | |
| film star (man): | | |
| film star (woman): | | |
| rock band: | | |
| singer (man): | | |
| singer (woman): | | |

*What do you think of ...?*

| | | |
|---|---|---|
| *I* | *love* | *him.* |
| | *(don't) like* | *her.* |
| | *hate* | *it.* |
| | *don't know* | *them.* |

| | | |
|---|---|---|
| *I think* | *he's* | *great.* |
| | *she's* | *wonderful.* |
| | *it's* | *horrible.* |
| | *they're* | |

**Tip**

**Be careful!**

What do you think of rap?
✓ I like **it**. ✗ ~~I like.~~

What do you think of Shakira?
✓ I like **her**. ✗ ~~I like she.~~

# 4D Swimming is my favourite activity!

## Reading

**1** Do the quiz. In pairs, compare your answers.

## Sports Quiz



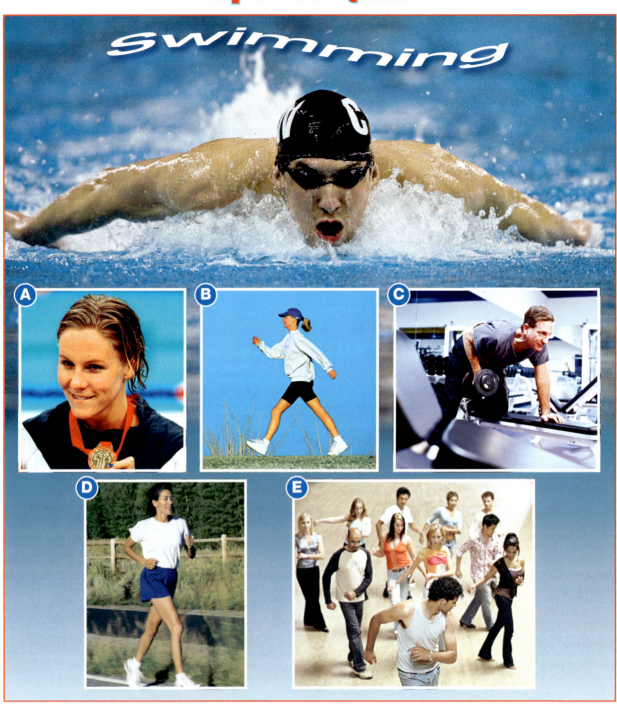

**Can you swim? Do you like swimming? What do you know about swimming?**

1 The number one sports activity in the world is **a** playing football. **b** swimming. **c** cycling.

2 Only one sport has more Olympic medals than swimming. Is it … **a** athletics? **b** boxing? **c** gymnastics?

3 Michael Phelps and Jenny Thompson swim for **a** Australia. **b** Britain. **c** the USA.

4 When you swim a kilometre in 30 minutes you use about **a** 200 calories. **b** 300 calories. **c** 400 calories.

2 Read the article to check your answers. Match the words in yellow and definitions 1–5. Do you agree that it is 'the perfect exercise'?

Swimming is the number one recreational activity in the world – yes, more people swim than play football or play golf or basketball!

It's very exciting to watch, too! Millions of TV fans watch the 34 swimming events at the Olympic Games. They love seeing swimmers like Americans Michael Phelps (six gold medals in Athens in 2004 and eight golds at the Beijing Olympics in 2008) and Jenny Thompson (12 Olympic medals, eight of them gold). Only athletics has more Olympic medals.

Swimming is an excellent way to exercise, relax and lose weight, too. Swimming for half an hour uses about 300 calories. It's the perfect exercise for all ages. Why don't you go swimming today?

1 An adjective: it means 'free time': ____________

2 An adjective + noun: what you get if you are first in an Olympic event: ____________

3 A verb + noun: for example, to go from 90 kilos to 70 kilos: ____________

4 A noun: people who love a sport, team, person, etc.: ____________

5 A noun: one of the competitions in a sports programme: ____________

## Speaking

3 Match the sentences and the photos in Exercise 1. Then tick (✓) the sentences you agree with.

1 Swimming is my favourite Olympic event. I'm a real fan. A

2 I hate dancing! But it's a good way to lose weight. ☐

3 My favourite recreational activity is walking. ☐

4 Weight training is good exercise, but really boring! ☐

5 I like doing a lot of different exercise, but I prefer running. ☐

4 In pairs, compare your ideas.

**A:** *I don't agree with number 2. I love dancing. I dance every weekend.*

**B:** *I agree with number 2. I like music, but I can't dance!*

## Grammar

5 Look at the sentences in Exercise 3 and complete the Grammar box.

**Verb + *-ing* for activities**

| | | Activity | |
|---|---|---|---|
| | | Learn _____ | English is great! |
| | | Do _____ | exercise is good. |
| I | hate | do _____ | homework. |
| My wife | loves | watch _____ | TV. |
| We | prefer | stay _____ | at home in the evening. |
| Do you | like | go _____ | to the cinema? |

AB, p. 103. Ex. 1 ▶

6 4.14 What do you like doing? Word Bank 13, p. 76.

## Speaking

7 4.15 In groups of three, listen to Kate and Anna talking. Tick (✓) what they like doing.
A: Tick (✓) the information about Anna.
B: Tick (✓) the information about Kate.
C: Tick (✓) the information about Leo.

| | | | | | |
|---|---|---|---|---|---|
| Anna | | | | | |
| Kate | | | | | |
| Leo | | | | | |

8 Talk about the information you have. What do Anna and Kate agree to do?

**A:** *Anna likes swimming. She loves ... .*

**B:** *Kate ... .*

**C:** *Leo ... .*

9 In groups, talk about your three favourite activities. Are they very similar?

**A:** *I love going to the gym, listening to music and cooking for my family. And you?*

# He goes running once a week

## Reading

**1** What do you think? Circle your opinion. In pairs, compare your opinions.

1 My weight is fine. I *need / don't need* to lose weight at the moment.
2 Going on a diet *is / isn't* very difficult for me.
3 I *eat / don't eat* a lot of junk food (burgers, hotdogs, chips, pizza, etc.).
4 I *prefer / don't prefer* eating lasagne to eating a salad.
5 Doing exercise *is / isn't* an important part of my life.
6 I *prefer / don't prefer* doing exercise to staying at home and watching TV.

**2** Look at the advert and Jim Ransom's photo. Which sentences from Exercise 1 do you think are his opinions, a) before and b) after his 'success story'?

## Listening

**3** 4.16 Listen to Jim and complete his personal details and weights in the advert.

**Naturlife**

***Before*** *– last year: _____ kg* ***After*** *– this year: _____ kg*

**Win $1000**

**Just tell us your success story about losing weight. Please send your details and photos!**

Name: *Jim Ransom*
Nationality: ____________
From: ____________
Lives: ____________
Age: ____________
Occupation: ____________

**4** Circle the correct verb. Listen to Jim again to check.

1 I *do / go / play* a lot of exercise.
2 I *do / go / play* tennis.
3 I *do / go / play* running.
4 I *do / go / play* swimming.
5 I *do / go / play* yoga.

**5** 4.17 Look at Jim's exercise calendar. How often does he do the activities? Write 1–4. Listen, check and repeat. Be careful with the 'silent' letters in every /ˈevri:/ and often /ˈɒfən/.

a ☐ once a week
b ☐ twice a week
c ☐ three times a week
d ☐ every other day

**Exercise calendar**

| Day | |
|---|---|
| Mon | (1) (2) |
| Tue | (3) |
| Wed | |
| Thur | |
| Fri | |
| Sat | (4) |
| Sun | |

## Grammar

**6** Look at Exercise 5 and complete the Grammar box.

**Frequency**

| | | | |
|---|---|---|---|
| How often | do | I/you/we/they | play ...? go ...? do ...? ...? |
| | does | he/she/it | |

| | | |
|---|---|---|
| Once | a | day. |
| ________ | | week. |
| ________ times | | month. |
| Every | | year. |
| Never. | | |

**Tip**

**Remember to use:**
***play*** for games
***go*** for activities (verb + *-ing*)
***do*** for other physical activities

AB, p. 104. Ex. 2 ▶

**7** How often do you do these things? In groups, find the coincidences.

**A:** *I have English lessons twice a week.*

**B:** *Me, too.*

**A:** *I read the newspaper ... .*

**B:** *Really? I ... .*

## Speaking

**8** Jim's friend Carmen isn't happy about his lifestyle. So she tries to find help. Read her message to Dr Sane's 'Solutions' page. What does Carmen think the problem is?

**Solutions to difficult problems!**

**Q: Crazy about exercise**

My friend Jim never stops exercising, and I don't think that's normal! Can you help him?
Carmen

**A: Dr Sane's answer**

Dear Carmen

It's good to go running or swimming often, to do sit-ups regularly and to play a ball game.

It's healthy to do aerobics sometimes and some weight training (1) ☐, too.

But tell your friend that it's important to do other things, too:

Here are my suggestions to him:

- Go to the cinema (2) ☐ and watch a different type of film each time.
- Listen to music every day – classical music at least (3) ☐.
- Go dancing with friends (4) ☐.
- Spend (5) ☐ with your family or friends – watch a good DVD together or have a special dinner.
- And remember to say 'I love you' (6) ☐.

**9** (4.18) Read Dr Sane's answer. In pairs, decide where to put these expressions in the text. Listen and check.

| | |
|---|---|
| **a** once a week | **d** once or twice a week |
| **b** one evening a week | **e** every other weekend |
| **c** once a day | **f** once a month |

**10** In pairs, ask and answer about the activities underlined in the text. Compare your answers to Dr Sane's suggestions. Do you have a healthy mind in a healthy body?

**A:** *How often do you ...?* **B:** ... .

# 4F We hardly ever go to bed early

## Listening

**1** 4.19 Leo, Anna, Kate and Tim want to see a film. Listen and complete the sentences.

1 ________ wants to see *Casablanca* at the ABC.
2 ________ doesn't like black and white films.
3 ________ doesn't remember who Judi Dench is.
4 ________ doesn't like Shakespearean actresses.
5 ________ makes a joke about beautiful actresses.
6 They agree to go and see the new ________ ________ film.

**2** Listen again. Number the sentences in the order that you hear them, 1–5.

A [ ] *I love them!*
B [*1*] *I don't like (   ) very much.*
C [ ] *I really like her!*
D [ ] *I hate them!*
E [ ] *Who's she?*

Match the sentences with the people or things they refer to. Write A–E.

[B] Casablanca  [ ] Keira Knightley  [ ] Judi Dench  [ ] Shakespearean actresses  [ ] Thrillers

## Speaking

**3** Get cards from your teacher. In groups, find out how much people know about Britain's famous:

- people (actors and actresses, singers, writers, etc.)
- places (monuments, shops, etc.)
- works of art (books, films, plays, etc.)
- bands

Who is the 'expert' in your group?

*What do you know about ...?*

*He's / She's / It's / They're a(n) ... . OR Who (are they)? I don't know him / her / it / them.*

*What do you think of him / her / it / them?*

*I love / (don't) like / hate / don't really know him / her / it / them.*
*I think he's ... . / she's ... . / it's ... . / they're ... .*

## Grammar

**4** Read about two couples talking about their weekends. Circle the correct option.

1 Which couple prefer TV to the cinema? *Debby and Justin / Sue and Roger*
2 Which couple love exercise and are always very busy? *Debby and Justin / Sue and Roger*
3 Who loves cooking? *Debby and Justin / Sue and Roger*

**5** 4.20 Read the texts again and complete with *in*, *on*, *at* or *to*. Listen and check. Then complete the Grammar box with the correct prepositions.

We're Debby and Justin. We usually spend our evenings and weekends (1)_____ home. We go (2)_____ the cinema about once a month, but we prefer watching TV, so we rent a lot of DVDs. We usually watch musicals and adventure films, and we like listening (3)_____ pop music. We hardly ever go out, but we sometimes eat (4)_____ a restaurant (5)_____ weekends. We hardly ever go (6)_____ bed late. We have friends, but we don't often see them. They're always busy!

Our names are Roger and Sue. We're often (17)_____ home (18)_____ the weekend and (19)_____ the evening. We like reading and listening (20)_____ music. We love opera and classical music, but we also listen (21)_____ a lot of rock music. We have a lot of friends, and (22)_____ Saturday morning, we sometimes go running with them. (23)_____ the evening, we sometimes go (24)_____ the cinema – about once a month – and we watch comedies and thrillers. We usually go (25)_____ bed early, (26)_____ about 10.30. Every Sunday we have a big lunch with our children and grandchildren, and their friends. We love cooking for them!

### Prepositions

**time: *at*, *in*, *on***

| | |
|---|---|
| ___ the morning(s)<br>the afternoon(s)<br>the evening (s) | ___ + days (Sundays)<br>+ parts of the day<br>(Sunday evenings) |
| ___ + time (six o'clock)<br>weekends<br>night | |

**place and movement: *at*, *to***

| Place | Movement |
|---|---|
| ___ home<br>a friend's house<br>a party<br>a disco | go ___ + place<br>(the cinema / a disco)<br>bed |

Go to Phrasebook 4 p. 78 ▶

Go to Essential Grammar 4 p. 119 ▶

**6** Complete the Grammar box with the yellow words in the texts. Put rules 1 and 2 in the correct order.

### Prepositions

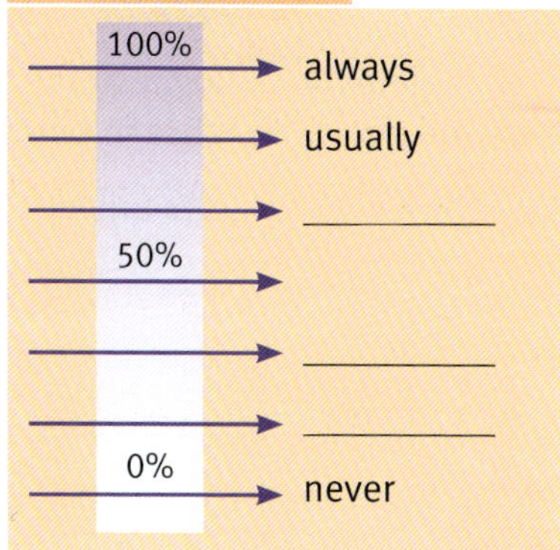


Rule 1: adverbs after *be* frequency go of the verb

Rule 2: frequency go of adverbs before other verbs

**7** Make true sentences with phrases 1–6 and adverbs from Exercise 6.

1 I ^don't often^ get up early on ^Sundays^
2 I take photos
3 I sing
4 I eat in restaurants
5 I'm at home on
6 I go to nightclubs

## Speaking

**8** Make notes about the places you usually go to and the things you often do at the weekend. Think about mornings, afternoons and evenings.

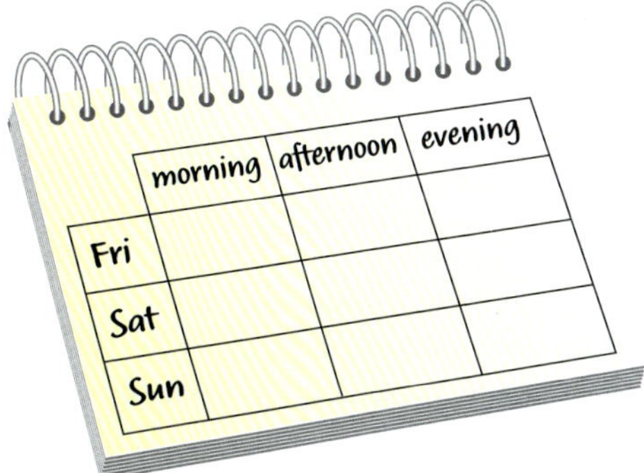


**9** Compare weekends with a partner.

**A:** *On Friday nights, I usually go out. And you?*

# Revision

4A **1** 4.21 Choose five words from Word Bank 12, p. 75. Listen and play BINGO! Tick (✓) the words you hear and say *Bingo!* when you have all five.

**2** 4.22 Complete the dialogue at the bus station. Listen and check. Practise in pairs.

**A:** Can I have two tickets to Bristol, please?

**B:** Single or (1)______________?

**A:** Return, please.

**B:** That's £82.00, (2)__________ .

**A:** Here (3)_____ are. What time (4)_______ it leave?

**B:** The next bus leaves (5)______ 8.05, from Gate 6.

**A:** What time does it (6)______________ in Bristol?

**B:** At 9.50.

**A:** (7)__________ you. Oh, where's Gate 6?

**B:** Over there. It's 8 o'clock now so ... you only have about four minutes!

4B **3** Talk about three people in your family.

**A:** *When's your ...'s birthday?*

**B:** *It's on ... .*

**A:** *What about your ...?*

**B:** *His / Her birthday is on ... .*

**4** Read the text and find the names of four groups who do not use the Gregorian calendar.

**When's New Year's Day?**

The year starts on 1st January, right? Well, not for everybody! Not everybody uses the Gregorian calendar. The calendars of the Chinese, Muslims and Jews, for example, are different. For them, the first day comes on a different date every year. Look at the chart below for the years 2009 to 2012.

| Calendar | 2009 | 2010 | 2011 | 2012 |
|---|---|---|---|---|
| Chinese | 26th January | | | |
| Islamic | | 7th December | | |
| Jewish | | | 29th September | 17th September |

Other groups use the same date every year. For example, Wiccans celebrate New Year's Eve on the evening of 31st October every year.

But, if the date is different, the message is the same. People all over the world say 'Happy New Year!'

**5** Get a card from your teacher. Complete more dates in the chart. Then in pairs, get the rest of the information.

**A:** *When does the Chinese year start in 2009?*

**B:** *On the twenty-sixth of January.*

4C **6** Join the words and make five true sentences. Tell a partner your five sentences. Give reasons. Are any of your sentences and reasons the same?

| | | |
|---|---|---|
| I | like / likes | action films<br>thrillers<br>adventure films |
| My sister / brother / partner | don't / doesn't like | cartoons<br>westerns |
| My flatmate / best friend | love / loves | science fiction |
| My parents | hate / hates | horror films<br>comedies<br>drama films |

**A:** *I like adventure films. I think they're exciting.*

**B:** *Me, too, but I prefer ... .*

**7** Complete the sentences with pronouns. Practice the dialogues in pairs.

**Ava:** Mmm! Orange juice! I love (1) *it*!

**Tina:** Me, too.

**Lea:** Do (2)_______ like *Guns N' Roses*?

**Nick:** No, I hate (3)_______.

**Ella:** Who's that woman? Do you know (4)_______?

**Anne:** Yes, I do. (5) _______'s my friend Amy.

**Rob:** Hi, Kim. Is your brother there? Can I speak to (6)_______?

**Kim:** Sorry, Rob. Mike isn't here. (7)_______'s at work.

**Jeff:** On Saturday afternoons my friends and I play football at the club. Come and play with (8)_______ this week.

**Sean:** Thanks, Jeff!

**Unit 4 Song:** *Under the bridge*, Red Hot Chili Peppers

To find the words, google lyric + the name of the song.

To find the video, google video + the name of the song and singer.

4D **8** 4.23 Listen and complete the chart for Pia. Use the emoticons.

☹☹ = hates ☹ = doesn't like ☺ = likes ☺☺ = loves

| | swimming | cycling | dancing | reading | shopping |
|---|---|---|---|---|---|
| Pia | | | | | |
| Your partner | | | | | |

**9** In pairs, ask and answer. Complete the table in Exercise 8.

**A:** *Do you like …ing?*

**B:** *No, I hate it.*

**10** Write three sentences about your partner using your information from Exercise 8.

*My partner really likes swimming, but she doesn't like cycling very much.*

4E **11** Look at Word Banks 6 and 9. In pairs, ask and answer *How often …?* and *Do you often …?* from the pictures. Try to learn five new things about your partner. Use the coloured routes in the chart to help you.

**A:** *How often do you … ?*

**B:** *Twice a week. / Never,* etc. *Do you often / sometimes … ?*

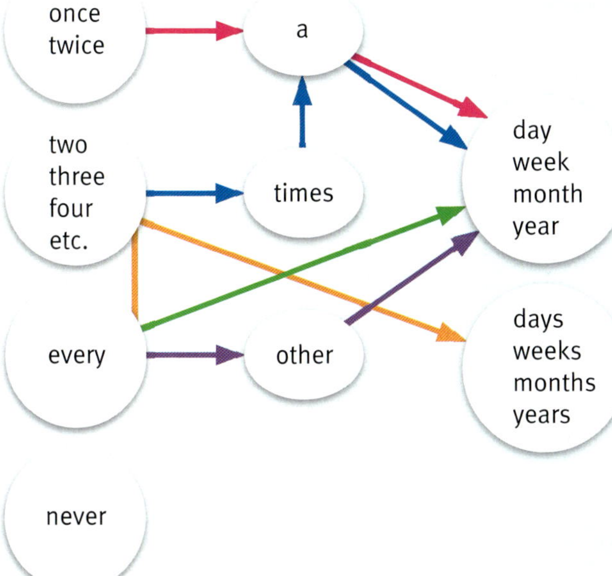


Go to **Writing 4** p. 63 ▶

**12** Play PINOCCHIO.
Get cards from your teacher. Find out who is not telling a true story.

4F **13** 4.24 Complete the dialogue. Listen and check.

**A:** What do you think of the *Arctic Monkeys*?

**B:** I (1) ______ them! I think they're the best band (2) ____ Britain.

**A:** Me, too. I think they're (3) ______________.

**C:** Well, I don't know (4) __________ .

**B:** Really? They're (5) ______ . And what do you (6) _________ of Diana Krall?

**C:** I (7) ________ her. She's an excellent jazz (8) ______________.

**A:** Who's (9) ______________? I don't know her. Is she American?

**14** In groups, ask and give opinions in the same way. Use the words in the box.

TV programmes actors bands and singers films soap operas politicians writers cities songs sports people

**15** Rewrite the sentences using the adverbs of frequency in brackets.

1 You're late. (often)

______________________________

2 They go for a run in the morning. (often)

______________________________

3 Chris goes shopping on Saturdays. (hardly ever)

______________________________

4 His classes are boring. (hardly ever)

______________________________

# Writing 1 Completing a form

**1** Look at this form for a language school. Underline 10 mistakes with CAPITAL LETTERS and spelling.

**MANCHESTER SCHOOL OF ENGLISH**

**Student**
Title: Mr / Mrs / Ms First name: *maria* Surname: *ivanov*
Nationality: *russian*
Passport / Identity card number: *917428863*
Job: *i'm a styudent of Economics at moscow State University.*
**Home address:**
House / flat number: *19*
Street: *Gogol Str, 27*
City: *moscow* Post code: *127106*
Country: *russia*
Phone number: *(007 95) 54968001*
Languages: *I speak russian and a little english.*
I want to learn English *for my job / to travel / to study / to translate / to meet people.*
Signature: *Maria Ivanov*

**Writing tip**

Use capital letters for names, countries, cities, nationalities, languages and the pronoun *I*.
*My name's* ***A****hmed. I'm* ***E****gyptian. I'm from* ***C****airo in* ***E****gypt and* ***I*** *speak* ***A****rabic and* ***E****nglish.*

**2** You're in Manchester to study English. Circle the correct options and complete the form. Be careful with CAPITAL LETTERS and spelling.

**MANCHESTER SCHOOL OF ENGLISH**

**Student**
Title: Mr / Mrs / Ms First name: ____________ Surname: ____________________________
Nationality: ____________
Passport / Identity card number: ____________
Job: ______________________________________________________________
**Home address:**
House / flat number: ________
Street: ___________________________________________________________
City: ___________________ Post code: ____________
Country: ___________________
Phone number: ___________________
Languages: ________________________________________________________
I want to learn English *for my job / to travel / to study / to translate / to meet people.*
Signature: ___________________

**3** Give your form to another student to check it for you.

**4** Give it to your teacher.

# An advert for an e-pal



**1** Read the advert and complete Haluk's information in the form. If you can't find the information, put a cross (✗).

## E-pal wanted to practise English!

Hi!

I'm Haluk Yilmaz and I'm Turkish. I'm 19 years old. I have two brothers and a sister. I live with my parents in a big flat in Ankara, the capital of Turkey.

I'm a student and I study Computer Science at Hacettepe University. I study English at a language school on Monday and Wednesday evenings, too. I need to practise my English because I want to travel.

At weekends, I usually play football. I like sports a lot. On Saturday evenings I go out with friends. We talk, dance, you know, typical students! On Sundays, I watch TV.

I smoke a little and I drink a lot of tea.

Please write to me!

Thanks! ☺

halukyilmaz@yahoo.com

**First name:** *Haluk* ____________
**Surname:** ____________
**Nationality:** ____________
**Age:** ______
**Marital Status:** ____________
**Family:** ___ brothers ___ sisters
**Home:** house / flat
**Who with?:** alone / with family / with friends
**Home town:** ____________
**Pets:** ______
**Occupation:** ____________
**Where?:** ____________
**Study English?:** Yes / No
**When:** ____________
**Why study English?** ____________

**Weekend activities:**
**Friday evening:** ____________
**Saturday:** ____________
**Sunday:** ____________
**Smoke:** Yes / No
**Drink:** ______

**2** Read the Writing tip and study the words in yellow in the advert in Exercise 1.
Match each example to a rule, 1–5.

a sister = rule 1 (one sister).

**Writing tip**

**The article**

1. Use *a* / *the* for singular nouns:
   a = one – *I have **a** dog.*
2. Use *a* + jobs:
   *I want to be **a** lawyer.*
3. Use *a* + *lot* / *little*:
   *I speak English **a** little.*
4. Use *the* to be specific = we know which noun:
   *I like music* = general
   *I like **the** music at this party* = specific
5. Don't use *the* for names:
   NOT ~~*the*~~ *Harvard University.*

**3** Write a similar advert about you. Give the information in the chart.
When you finish, compare all your sentences to Haluk's. Check each noun.

**a** Is it singular or plural?

**b** Does it need an article?

**4** Give your advert to another student to check it for you.

**5** Give it to your teacher.

# Writing 3 A composition

**1** Read the composition about Teresa.
Match the questions to the correct paragraph, 1–4.

### Somebody I like very much

**1** My mother's best friend is a wonderful woman. Her name's Teresa and she's Colombian. She comes from Medellin and is about 41. She lives with her sister in a small flat in Lynwood, Los Angeles.

**2** She gets up at 6 o'clock every day. She goes to work by bus. She arrives at work at 7.30. She's a chef. She makes breakfast, lunch and dinner.

**3** She usually leaves work at seven. In the evenings, she plays cards or watches TV. She doesn't go out a lot, but on Tuesdays she studies English. Her English is good now.

**4** I think she's great! She's strong and intelligent. Her life isn't easy, but she's always very positive. I know my mother loves her.

| | Paragraph |
|---|---|
| Why do you like her or him? | ☐ |
| Who is it? | ☐ |
| What does she or he do after work? | ☐ |
| What's her or his typical day? | ☐ |

**2** Complete these sentences with *and* or *but*.

1 My father drinks milk _____ orange juice, _____ he doesn't drink tea or coffee.

2 He has a car, _____ he always goes to work by train.

3 He gets up at 7 o'clock _____ has breakfast at home.

4 Spider-Man jumps high _____ runs up buildings, _____ he can't fly.

**3** Read and complete paragraph 4 of another student's composition with *he*, *he's*, *is* or *his*.

I think (1) *he's* a fantastic teacher. (2) _____ always helps (3) _____ students before and after (4) _____ classes. (5) _____ spends a lot of (6) _____ free time with them. (7) _____ works a lot, but (8) _____ never tired or negative. (9) _____ wonderful! I really like him.

**Writing tip**

Use *and* and *but* to make L-O-N-G sentences.
*Her name's Teresa, She's Colombian.*
→ *Her name's Teresa **and** she's Colombian.*

With *and* you don't need to repeat the pronoun.
*She comes from Medellín. She's about 35.*
→ *She comes from Medellín **and is** about 35.*

Use *but* to change direction.
− +
Her life isn't easy ***but*** she's always positive.

**4** Write a similar composition about somebody you like.

- ☐ Write four paragraphs to answer the questions in Exercise 1 in the correct order.
- ☐ Try to make long sentences with *and* or *but*.
- ☐ Use a bilingual dictionary for three or four new words if necessary.
- ☐ Read it again carefully. Check your use of *he*, *he's*, *his* OR *she*, *she's*, *her*.
- ☐ Give your composition to a friend to check it for you.

**5** Give it to your teacher.

# A blog entry

*Hi! This is Boris, from Berlin. Welcome to my blog page!*

My favourite part of the weekend is Saturday night. I work and study a lot from Monday to Friday, and on Friday evenings I'm really tired. I hardly ever go out.

But not on Saturdays! First I always meet friends for dinner, usually in a restaurant. Then we go dancing. I love it! Berlin has a lot of really good clubs and we go to a different place every weekend. I like all types of dance music, but I prefer fast techno. We often party all night and then go out for breakfast! As you can imagine, I don't do a lot on Sundays!

**1** Read Boris's blog. Write T (true) or F (false).

1. He's from Bonn. ___
2. His favourite part of the weekend is Saturday night. ___
3. On Saturday nights he often eats at a friend's house. ___
4. He usually goes dancing in different places. ___
5. He always gets home at about five in the morning. ___
6. He does a lot on Friday evenings and Sundays. ___

**2** How do you say the words in yellow in your language? Use a bilingual dictionary to check if necessary.

**Writing tip**

Use *First*, *Then*, *and then* to organise and connect your sentences.

**3** Complete the blog with *to*, *for*, *at* or *on*.

(1)_____ Friday evenings I finish work (2)_____ 5.30. First, we all usually go (3)_____ a drink together. Then I always stay at home and relax (4)_____ Friday nights. (5)_____ Saturday afternoons, I often go (6)_____ a football match. I support West Ham and I go (7)_____ all the games. Then (8)_____ Saturday evenings, I always go (9)_____ a run. And then I usually go (10)_____ a restaurant (11)_____ dinner with my girlfriend. That's my favourite part of the weekend. I usually go (12)_____ the cinema (13)_____ Sunday evenings or spend time online (14)_____ home.

**4** Complete the blog with the verbs in the correct form.

I love Saturday mornings. First I always (1) *go* (go) to the gym to (2)_____ (do) exercise. I love (3)_____ (do) weight-training and (4)_____ (listen) to rock music on my MP3 player.

Then I sometimes go (5)_____ (shop) with my family, but I prefer (6)_____ (go) with my friends. I don't like (7)_____ (shop) online.

But my favourite part of the weekend is Sunday mornings. My children (8)_____ (go) to the park, my husband (9)_____ (go) shopping and then I (10)_____ (be) finally alone! I (11)_____ (read) the newspapers and then (12)_____ (do) yoga for an hour. It's wonderful.

**5** Write a blog entry about your favourite part of the weekend.

- Use the models in Exercises 1, 3 and 4 to help you.
- Try to organise your sentences with *First*, *Then*, *and then*.
- When you finish, check your use of prepositions.
- Check you have *-ing* forms after the verbs *like*, *love*, *hate* and *prefer*.
- Give your blog to a friend to check it for you.

**6** Give it to your teacher.

# Word Bank 1 Numbers

## A

1.5 Listen and say the numbers. Cover the words and test yourself.

| 1 | 2 | 3 | 4 | 5 | 6 | 7 | 8 | 9 | 10 | 11 | 12 |
|---|---|---|---|---|---|---|---|---|---|---|---|
| one | two | three | four | five | six | seven | eight | nine | ten | eleven | twelve |

## B

1.26 Complete numbers 13–29. Listen, check and repeat.

| | | | | | |
|---|---|---|---|---|---|
| $13 | thirteen dollars | £17 | _ _ _ _ nteen pounds | 21 | _ _ enty-_ _ _ |
| 14c | _ _ urteen cents | 18p | _ _ _ _ teen pence | 22 | _ _ _ _ _ _ _-two |
| €15 | _ _ fteen euros | ¥19 | _ _ _ _ teen yen | 23 | _ _ _ _ _ _ _-_ _ _ _ _ |
| 16c | _ _ _ teen cents | 20 | _ wenty | 29 | _ _ _ _ _ _ _-_ _ _ _ |

## C

1.28 Complete the high numbers. Listen, check and repeat. Cover the words and test yourself.

20 twenty
30 thirty
40 _ _ rty
50 _ _ _ ty
60 _ _ _ ty
70 _ _ _ _ _ ty
80 _ _ _ _ ty
90 _ _ _ _ ty
100 a hundred
101 a _ _ _ _ _ _ _ and _ _ _
200 two hundred
311 _ _ _ _ _ hundred and eleven
428 four _ _ _ _ _ _ _ and twenty-eight
567 _ _ _ _ _ _ _ _ _ _ _ and sixty-seven
999 _ _ _ _ _ _ _ _ _ _ _ _ _ _ _ _ _ _ _ _ _ _ _ _ _
1,000 a thousand
2001 two _ _ _ _ sand and one
456,789 four hundred and _ _ _ _ _-_ _ _
_ _ _ _ _ _ _ _ _, _ _ _ _ _ hundred and _ _ _ _ _ _ _-_ _ _ _
1,000,000 a million
10,000,000 _ _ _ million

1F p.14

# Classroom instructions

**1** 1.11 Match the words and the pictures. Listen and check.

| | | | |
|---|---|---|---|
| ☐ close (your book) | ☐ open (your book) | ☐ listen to (the CD) | ☑ 1 read (the text) |
| ☐ look at (the book) | ☐ say (the words) | ☐ match (the word and picture) | ☐ write (the word) |

**2** Complete the sentences with three of the verbs from Exercise 1.

1 ______________ the pictures.

2 ______________ the exercise on your CD.

3 ______________ your name on the page.

**3** Test your partner. Student A: Say a picture number. Student B: Say the phrase.

**A:** Picture number six?

**B:** Match the word and picture. Picture eight?

**A:** Open your book.

1B p.7

# Word Bank 3 Personal things

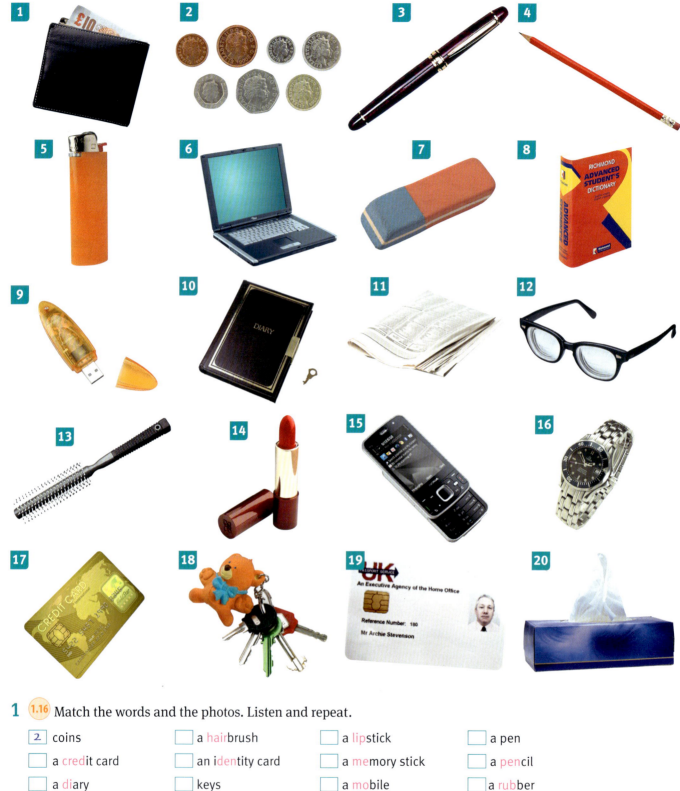

**1** 1.16 Match the words and the photos. Listen and repeat.

| | | | |
|---|---|---|---|
| 2 coins | ☐ a hairbrush | ☐ a lipstick | ☐ a pen |
| ☐ a credit card | ☐ an identity card | ☐ a memory stick | ☐ a pencil |
| ☐ a diary | ☐ keys | ☐ a mobile | ☐ a rubber |
| ☐ a dictionary | ☐ a laptop | ☐ a newspaper | 1 a wallet |
| ☐ glasses | ☐ a lighter | ☐ tissues | ☐ a watch |

**2** Cover the words and test your partner. Point at the objects.

**A:** *What's this? / What are these?*

**B:** *It's a(n) ... . / They're ... .*

1C p.9

# Countries and nationalities

**1** 1.21 Write *Africa*, *the Americas*, *Asia*, *Europe* or *Oceania*.
Write one more country. Draw the flag and write the nationality. Listen and check.

**2** Cover the countries and nationalities. In pairs, point to a flag and test your partner.

**A:** *What country's this?*

**B:** *(I think) it's ... . / I don't know. What is it?*

| ______________ | | | Languages |
|---|---|---|---|
| | Argentina | Argentinian | |
| | Brazil | Brazilian | Portuguese |
| | Mexico | Mexican | |
| | The USA | American | |
| | | | |

| ______ and ______ | | | Languages |
|---|---|---|---|
| | China | Chinese | |
| | Japan | Japanese | |
| | India | Indian | Hindi/Urdu/English |
| | Australia | Australian | |
| | | | |

| ______________ | | | Languages |
|---|---|---|---|
| | Britain | British | |
| | France | French | |
| | Spain | Spanish | |
| | Italy | Italian | |
| | Germany | German | |
| | | | |

| ______________ | | | Languages |
|---|---|---|---|
| | Egypt | Egyptian | Arabic |
| | South Africa | South African | E________ |
| | | | |

1D p.11

## Languages

**1** 2.15 Write the languages of each country. Mark the stress with a circle. Listen and check.

**2** What languages do you speak?

**Tip**

I (don't) speak Russian (very) well.

NOT ~~I speak very well English.~~

I speak (a little) English = I speak English (a little).

Use CAPITAL LETTERS for countries, nationalties and languages.

# Jobs

**1** 1.25 Match the words and the pictures. Listen and check.

- [ ] an actor / an actress
- [ ] a businessman / a businesswoman
- [ ] a chef
- [ ] a civil servant
- [ ] a dentist
- [ ] a doctor
- [ ] an engineer
- [ ] a footballer
- [ ] a housewife
- [ ] a journalist
- [ ] a lawyer
- [ ] a police officer
- [ ] a receptionist
- [ ] a secretary
- [1] a student
- [ ] a teacher
- [ ] a waiter and a waitress
- [ ] unemployed
- [ ] retired
- 20 ________

**2** Tick (✓) words which are similar in your language.

**3** Write another job in number 20 and draw a picture for it.

# English vowel sounds

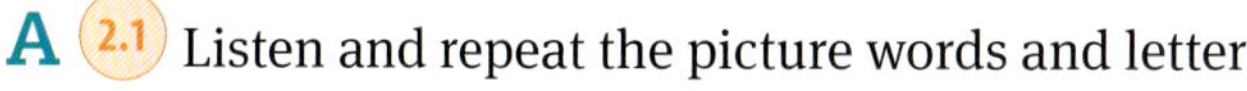

**A** 2.1 Listen and repeat the picture words and letters. 2A p.18

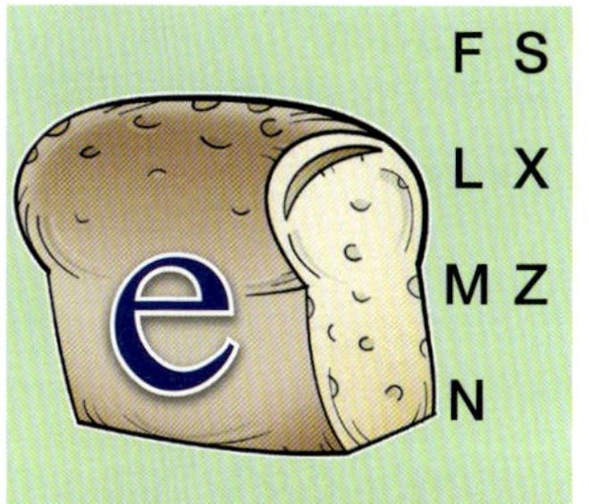


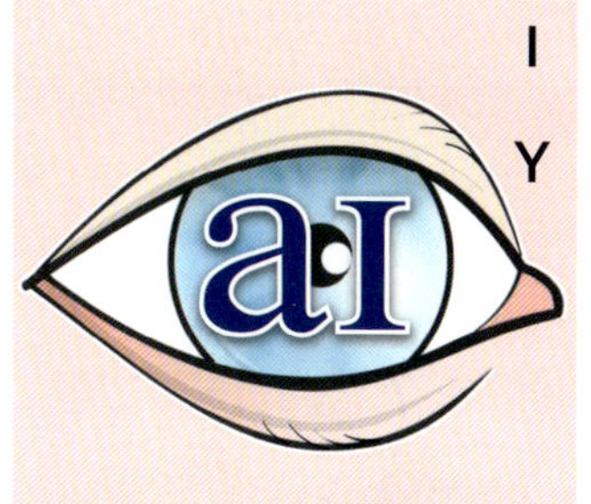

**B** 2.28 Listen and repeat eight pairs of picture words. Each pair has the same sound. 2R p.31

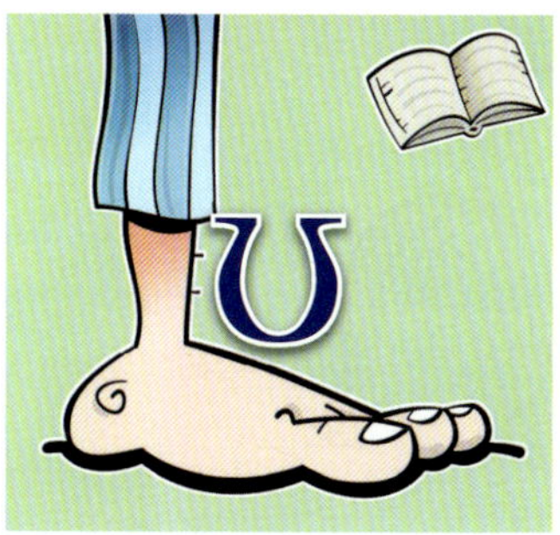

**C** 3.23 Listen and repeat five more pairs of picture words. Each pair has the same sound. 3R p.44

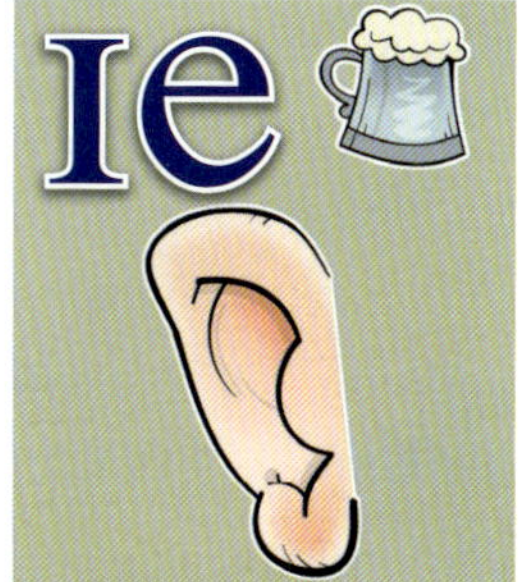

How many vowel sounds does English have? Does your language have all these sounds?

# Word Bank 7 Your family

**1** 2.10 Imagine this is your family tree. You are ME. Match the pictures and words, 1–12. Listen and check.

| | | | | | | | | | |
|---|---|---|---|---|---|---|---|---|---|
| ☐ | my brother | ☐ | my children | ☐ | my daughter | ☐ | my father | ☐ | my grandfather |
| ☐ | my grandmother | 7 | my grandparents | ☐ | my husband or wife | ☐ | my mother | ☐ | my parents |
| ☐ | my sister | 5 | my son | | | | | | |

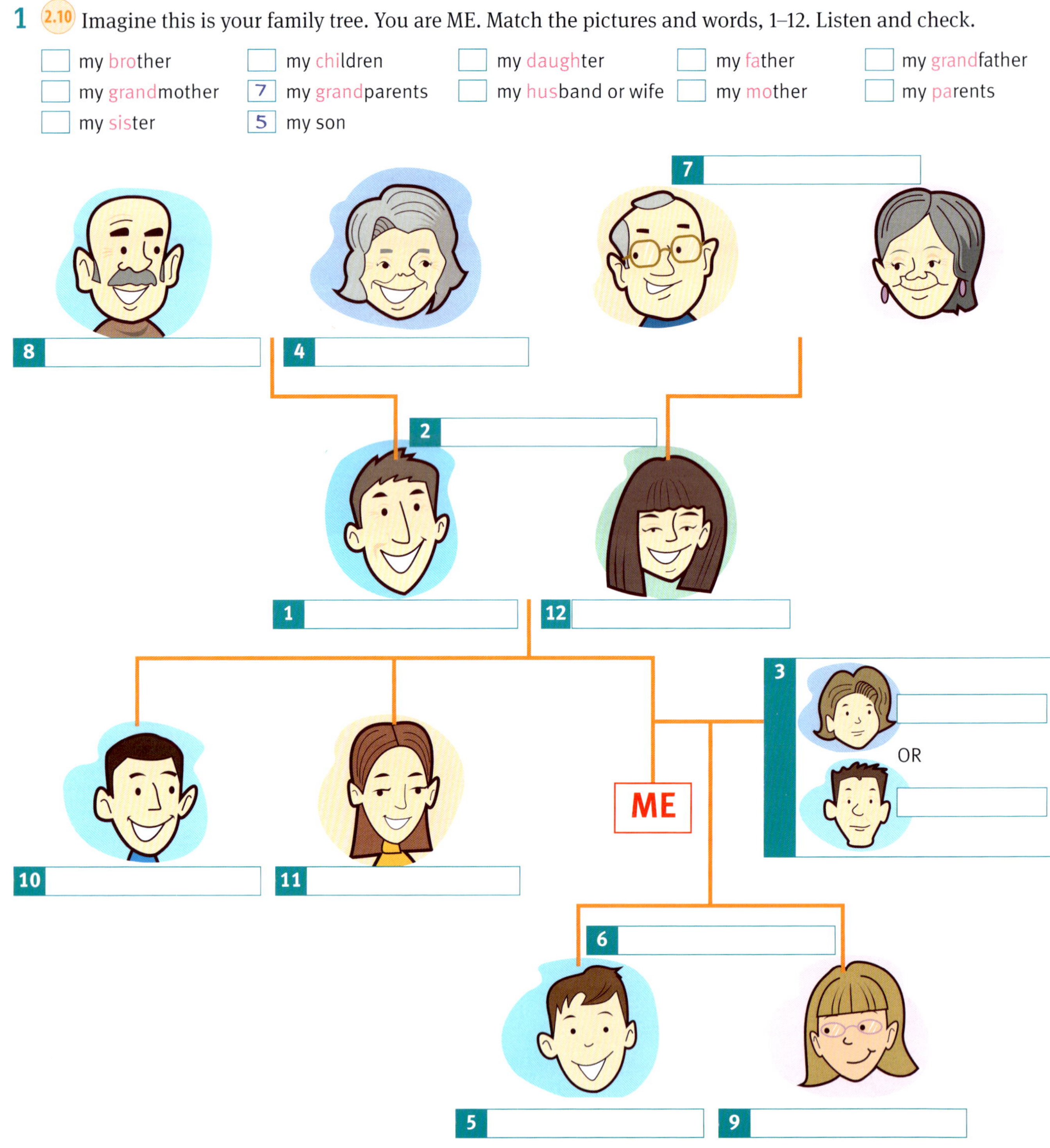


**2** What is the common vowel sound?

1 *brother, husband, mother, son*

2 *children, sister*

3 *father, parents, children, husband*

**3** Write the names of *your* family in the boxes in Exercise 1. If you don't have a brother, sister or children, leave those boxes empty. If you have more, draw more boxes.

**4** In pairs, introduce your family. Say their names and ages.

**A:** *This is my grandfather. His name is Jorge. He's 82. He's alive.*

**B:** *I'm not married and I don't have a son or a daughter.*

**Tip**

If you get married, you get 'in-laws':
mother-in-law
father-in-law, etc.

2D p.24

**1** 2.22 Match the 'go' phrases and pictures, 1–7. Listen and check.

☐ go to the beach ☐ go to the cinema ☐ go to a nightclub ☐ go to a restaurant
[1] go for a walk / go for a run ☐ go out with friends ☐ go shopping

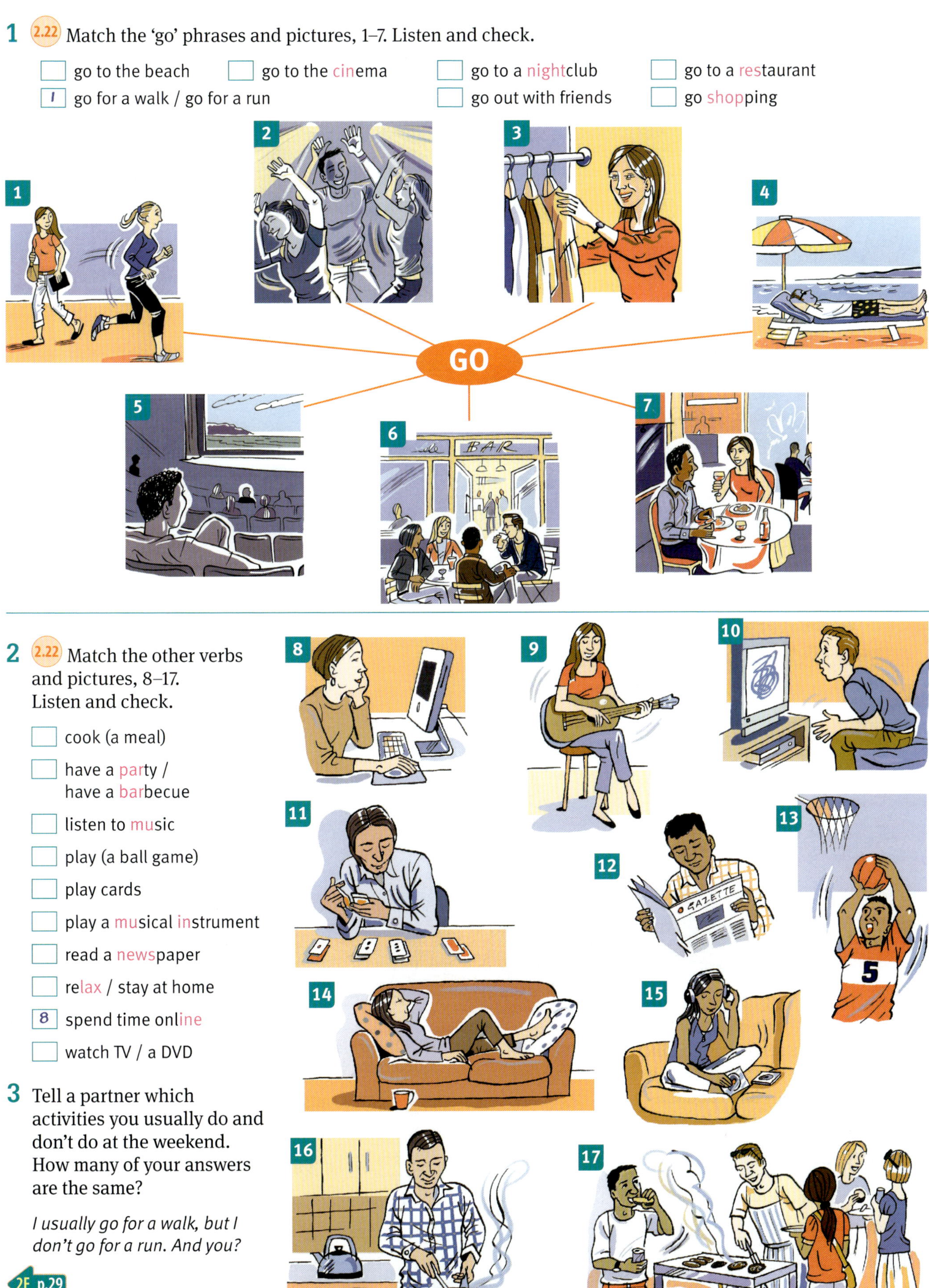


**2** 2.22 Match the other verbs and pictures, 8–17. Listen and check.

- ☐ cook (a meal)
- ☐ have a party / have a barbecue
- ☐ listen to music
- ☐ play (a ball game)
- ☐ play cards
- ☐ play a musical instrument
- ☐ read a newspaper
- ☐ relax / stay at home
- [8] spend time online
- ☐ watch TV / a DVD

**3** Tell a partner which activities you usually do and don't do at the weekend. How many of your answers are the same?

*I usually go for a walk, but I don't go for a run. And you?*

2F p.29

# Word Bank 9 Adjectives

**1** (3.4) Match the sentences and pictures, 1–9. Which two sentences are good excuses to say 'no' to an invitation? Listen and check.

- [ ] We're bored.
- [ ] We're cold.
- [ ] I'm hungry.
- [ ] We're late!
- [ ] We're (very) tired!
- [1] I'm busy.
- [ ] I'm hot.
- [ ] We're ill.
- [ ] I'm (really) thirsty.

3A p.33

**2** Match the suggestions and the sentences in Exercise 1.

a [ ] Yes! Let's call a taxi.
b [ ] Me, too. Let's have a glass of water.
c [ ] OK. Let's have a sandwich.
d [ ] Well, let's play football.
e [ ] Let's stop and go home.
f [1] Sorry, no problem. Can I call you again tomorrow?

# The time

**1** (3.14) What's the time? Look at the clock below. In pairs, complete the times, 1–11. Listen and check.

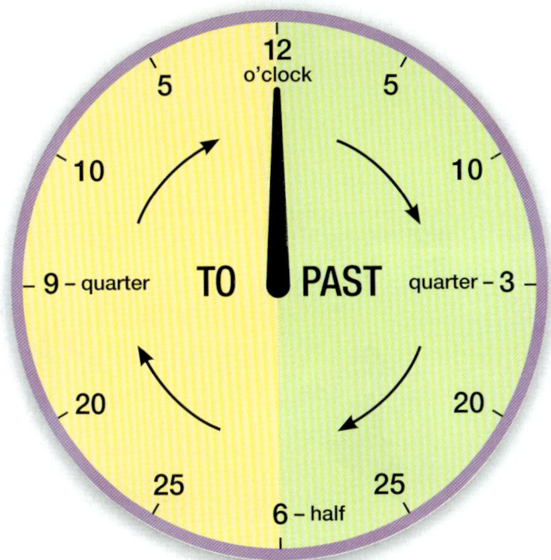


1 **8.00** It's eight o'clock.
2 **8.15** It's eight fifteen. = It's quarter _past_ eight.
3 **8.20** It's eight twenty. = It's twenty ________ eight.
4 **8.30** It's eight thirty. = It's half ________ eight.
5 **8.35** It's eight thirty-five. = It's twenty ________ nine.
6 **8.45** It's eight forty-five. = ___ quarter ________ nine.
7 **9.10** It's nine ten. = ______ ______ past nine.
8 **9.15** It's nine fifteen. = ______ ______ past nine.
9 **9.30** It's nine thirty. = ______ ______ past nine.
10 **9.45** It's nine forty-five. = ______ ______ to ten.
11 **10.00** It's ten ________ .

**2** Cover the words and test yourself.
Can you say all the times in one minute?

**3** Complete with time words.

1 60 _seconds_ = a minute
2 60 ________ = an hour
3 24 ________ = a day
4 7 ________ = a week
5 4 ________ = a month
6 12 ________ = a year

**4** Learn the time expressions.

| |
|---|
| today |
| tonight |
| tomorrow |
| yesterday |

| | |
|---|---|
| in | the morning |
| | the afternoon |
| | the evening |
| at | night |

| | |
|---|---|
| every | day |
| | week |
| | month |
| | year |

| | |
|---|---|
| this | week |
| next | weekend |
| last | year |

| | |
|---|---|
| tomorrow | morning |
| yesterday | afternoon |
| | evening |

3D p38

# Word Bank 11 Everyday activities

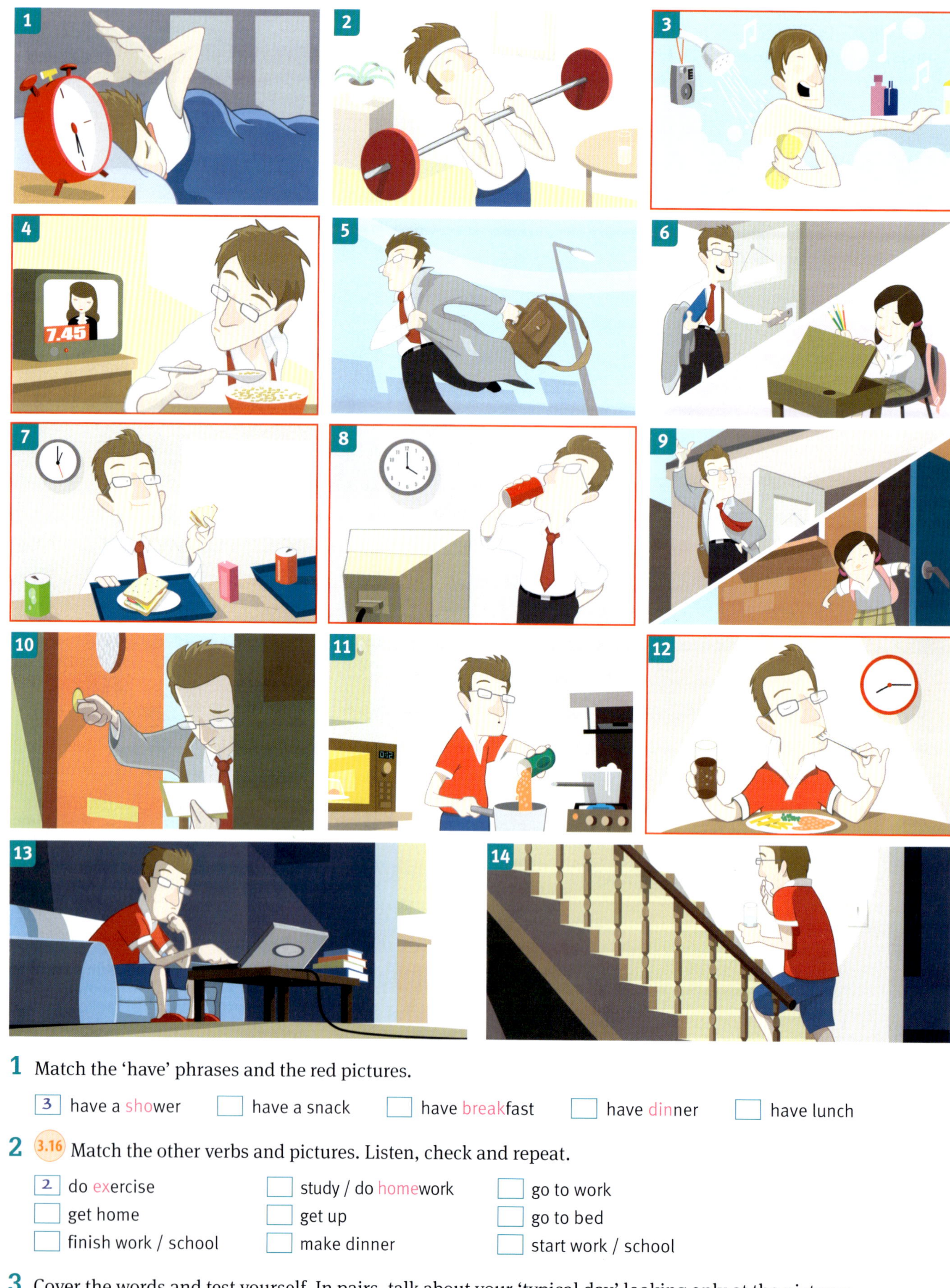


**1** Match the 'have' phrases and the red pictures.

[3] have a shower  [ ] have a snack  [ ] have breakfast  [ ] have dinner  [ ] have lunch

**2** 3.16 Match the other verbs and pictures. Listen, check and repeat.

| | | |
|---|---|---|
| [2] do exercise | [ ] study / do homework | [ ] go to work |
| [ ] get home | [ ] get up | [ ] go to bed |
| [ ] finish work / school | [ ] make dinner | [ ] start work / school |

**3** Cover the words and test yourself. In pairs, talk about your 'typical day' looking only at the pictures.

3E p.40

# Around town Word Bank 12

**1** 4.1 Match the words and the places 1–12. Listen and check.

| | | | |
|---|---|---|---|
| [ ] a cinema | [ ] a language school | [ ] a restaurant | [ ] a supermarket |
| [ ] an airport | [ ] a hotel | [ ] a nightclub | [1] a travel agent's |
| [ ] a flat | [ ] a gym | [ ] an office | [ ] a (sports) club |

13

**2** 4.1 Match the words and the places 13–27. Listen and check.

| | | | | |
|---|---|---|---|---|
| [ ] a café | [ ] a museum | [13] an art gallery | [ ] a park | [ ] a palace |
| [ ] a castle | [ ] a shopping centre | [ ] a theatre | [ ] a university | [ ] a station |
| [ ] a monument | [ ] a bank | [ ] a bus station | [ ] a post office | [ ] a pub |

**3** How many places on this page are similar in your language? Compare with a partner.

**A:** *In Spanish, for airport, we say 'aeropuerto'.*

**4** Cover the words and test your partner. Can you remember all 27 places on this page?

# Word Bank 13 Free-time activities

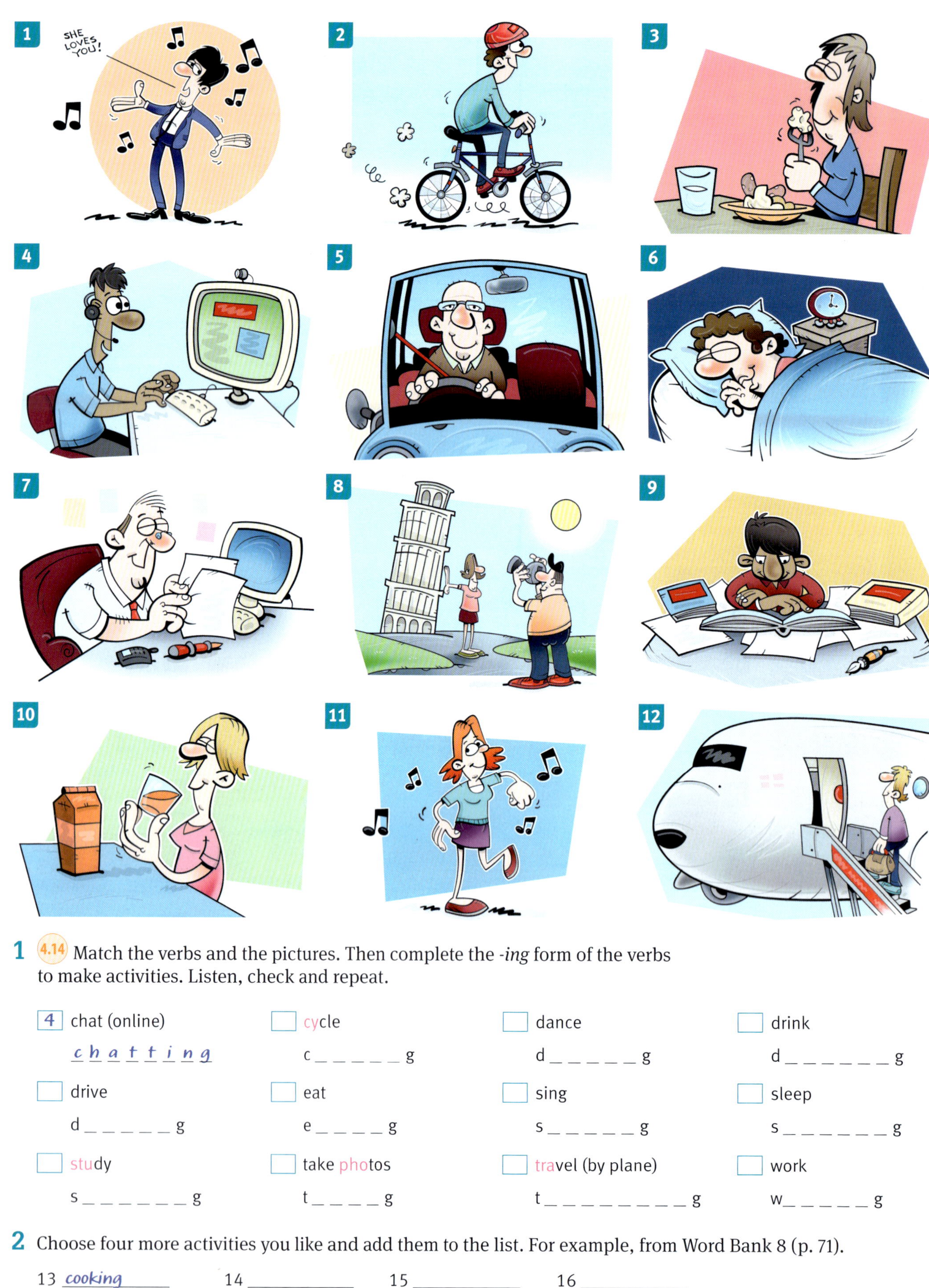


**1** (4.14) Match the verbs and the pictures. Then complete the *-ing* form of the verbs to make activities. Listen, check and repeat.

| | | | |
|---|---|---|---|
| [4] chat (online) | [ ] cycle | [ ] dance | [ ] drink |
| chatting | c _ _ _ _ _ g | d _ _ _ _ _ g | d _ _ _ _ _ _ g |
| [ ] drive | [ ] eat | [ ] sing | [ ] sleep |
| d _ _ _ _ _ g | e _ _ _ _ g | s _ _ _ _ _ g | s _ _ _ _ _ _ g |
| [ ] study | [ ] take photos | [ ] travel (by plane) | [ ] work |
| s _ _ _ _ _ _ g | t _ _ _ _ g | t _ _ _ _ _ _ _ _ g | w _ _ _ _ _ g |

**2** Choose four more activities you like and add them to the list. For example, from Word Bank 8 (p. 71).

13 cooking ______ 14 ______ 15 ______ 16 ______

4D p.53

## Unit 1

**1** P.1 Listen. How do you say these phrases in your language? Translate the phrases in pencil.

| English | Your language |
|---|---|
| I'm OK. / Are you OK? | |
| I think ... | |
| I agree. | |
| Hi. / Hello. | |
| Nice to meet you, (too). | |
| Bye. / Goodbye. | |
| I don't know. | |
| I don't remember. | |
| Excuse me, please. | |
| I'm sorry. | |
| Come in. | |
| Sorry I'm late. | |
| That's OK. | |
| Just a moment, please. | |
| Thank you. | |
| You're welcome. | |
| Where (in the USA) are you from? | |
| Congratulations! | |
| Wow! That's interesting! | |
| See you. | |
| We're (not) married. | |
| I'm single. | |
| No way! | |

**2** Cover the translations and test yourself. Can you remember the meaning in your language?

**3** Cover the English. Look at your translations. Can you remember the phrases in English?

## Unit 2

**1** Erase the translations in Unit 1 you don't need now.

**2** P.2 Listen. How do you say these phrases in your language? Translate them in pencil.

| English | Your language |
|---|---|
| How do you spell that? | |
| Is that right? | |
| Yes, you're right. | |
| Sorry, you're wrong. | |
| No problem. | |
| Would you like a drink? | |
| Yes, please. | |
| No, thanks. | |
| Here you are. | |
| How old are you? | |
| How many? | |
| Well done. | |
| Me, too. | |
| Sorry? | |
| Oh, really? | |
| I see ... | |
| How nice! | |
| A little. | |
| A lot. | |
| (Not) very well. | |
| Great! | |
| What about you? | |
| Of course! | |
| Have a good holiday. | |
| Thank you very much. | |
| What else? | |

**3** Listen to your CD regularly and translate the phrases in Units 1 and 2 in your mind. Can you remember them all?

# Phrasebook

## Unit 3

**1** Erase the translations in Units 1 and 2 you don't need now.

**2** P.3 Listen. How do you say these phrases in your language? Translate them in pencil.

| English | Your language |
|---|---|
| Can I speak to Paul, please? | |
| This is Paul. | |
| Hi, Paul. It's Carmen. | |
| Listen, ... | |
| My turn. | |
| Ready? | |
| Sure. | |
| Try again. | |
| That's a great idea. | |
| Perfect! | |
| Right, then. | |
| See you later. | |
| Well, ... | |
| Sorry, not just now. | |
| It's an emergency. | |
| It's the same in my language. | |
| For example, ... | |
| I think so. | |
| I don't think so. | |
| You mean ...? | |
| Don't miss it! | |
| Let's go. | |
| It's for you. | |
| Wait a minute! | |

## Unit 4

**1** Test yourself on Units 1, 2 and 3. Erase the translations you don't need now.

**2** P.4 Listen. How do you say these phrases in your language? Translate them in pencil.

| English | Your language |
|---|---|
| Can I help you? | |
| Would you like (a single or a return)? | |
| How much is it? | |
| What time does the next train (to London) leave? | |
| Just a second. | |
| Anything else? | |
| ... you see. | |
| No idea. | |
| What do you think of (her)? | |
| I love it. | |
| I hate them. | |
| I prefer (football). | |
| No, not really. | |
| How often do you (come here)? | |
| Come on! | |
| Only joking! | |
| Have a good trip. | |
| What's up? | |
| I'm not sure. | |
| I have no idea. | |

# Nice to meet you!



## Vocabulary

**Nouns:** an actor, an actress, an airport, a book, a city, an exercise, a film, a hotel, a name, a party, a photo, a restaurant, a supermarket, a TV programme

**Adjectives:** bad, excellent, fantastic, good, OK, terrible

**Articles:** a, an

**Expressions:** Hi. Hello. I'm … . I think … . My name's … . Nice to meet you, (too). No. … . Yes, I agree.

**1** Complete with *a* or *an*.

1 *a* party
2 ___ restaurant
3 ___ airport
4 ___ actor
5 ___ book
6 ___ city
7 ___ English book
8 ___ actress
9 ___ exercise
10 ___ supermarket

p.5 **2** Make sentences with *It's a …* or *It's an …* .

1 hotel (excellent)
*It's an excellent hotel.*
2 supermarket (OK)
It's ______________.
3 film (excellent)
______________.
4 exercise (terrible)
______________.
5 photo (fantastic)
______________.
6 TV programme (bad)
______________.

**3** Complete the sentences with one word.

1 The Meridien's an *excellent* hotel.
2 The *Lord of the Rings* is a fantastic ________ .
3 'Big Brother's' ________ good TV programme.
4 I think Arnold Schwarzenegger's a bad ________.
5 I ______ Carrefour's an OK supermarket.
6 Nice to ________ you.

**4** (1.1) Put the words in the correct order. Listen and check.

1 Angelina Jolie / good / a / actress / 's
*Angelina Jolie's a good actress.*
2 an / party / 's / it / OK
______________
3 fantastic / 's / Sydney / city / a
______________
4 is / book / excellent / an / *The Little Prince*
______________
5 bad / Paulo's / a / think / I / is / restaurant
______________
6 's / meet / too / nice / to / you / it
______________

**5** Use *I think* … and write your opinion about:

Cate Blanchett Pizza Hut *Titanic*
*Friends* the Hilton Carrefour

1 *I think Carrefour is a good supermarket.*
2 ______________
3 ______________
4 ______________
5 ______________
6 ______________

### Study tip

**International words**

1 Underline the nouns and adjectives in the Vocabulary box that are similar in your language.
2 Listen to the words on your Student CD.
3 Practise the stress and pronunciation of the words in English.

# I'm fine, thanks

## Vocabulary

**Word Bank 1:** Numbers 1–12 p. 64

**Word Bank 2:** Classroom instructions p. 65

**Nouns:** an aspirin, a class, a picture, a teacher

**Expressions:** Good morning. Good afternoon. Good evening. Good night. Goodbye. Bye. See you. (I'm) Sorry. I don't remember. What's your name? Come in. How are you? Are you OK? I'm fine, (thanks)! And you? Just a moment. (Sorry) I'm late. That's OK. Right!

p.7

**1** Write the contractions.

1 I am a teacher.

*I'm a teacher.* ______

2 You are an excellent singer.

______

3 I am not an actress.

______

4 You are not a bad actor.

______

5 I am sorry.

______

6 I am fine, thanks. And you?

______

**2** Write the opposite of sentences 1–4 in Exercise 1.

1 *I'm not a teacher.* ______
2 ______
3 ______
4 ______

**3** Complete the word web with the nouns. Use Word Bank 2, p. 65, to help you.

1 the sentences
2 the photos
3 the words
4 the dialogue
5 your teacher
6 the pictures

read: 1, ___, ___
write: 1, ___, ___
listen to: 1, ___, ___, ___
complete: 1, 3, 4 ✓
look at: 1, ___, ___, ___, ___, ___
match: 1, ___, ___, ___, ___

**4** (1.2) Listen. Tick (✓) the phrases you hear in the word web in Exercise 3.

**5** Complete the dialogues.

1 **Laura:** Are you John Simpson?
**John:** Yes, ______ ______ .
**Laura:** I'm Laura Wood. Nice ______ ______ ______ .

2 **Student:** Sorry ______ late. Can I come in?
**Teacher:** ______ OK, Lars. Come ______ .

3 **Carol:** How ______ ______, Edward?
**Edward:** ______ ______, thanks. And you?
**Carol:** I'm fine, too.

4 **Teacher:** Good ______, class! ______ ______ ready?
**Student:** ______ ______ moment, Mrs Brooks.

**6** Put the words in the correct order. Use CAPITAL letters, full stops (.) and question marks (?).

1 ok that's *That's OK.*
2 a just moment ______
3 i'm late sorry ______
4 i come in can ______
5 don't i remember ______

**7** Write the answers.

1 What's one + two + nine – seven – four + ten – eight + three + six?

______

2 What's twelve – seven + one – five + eleven – four + two?

______

3 What's ten + one – two + three – five + four – seven + eight – six?

______

# What's this in English?



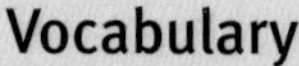

## Vocabulary

**Word Bank 3:** Personal things p. 66

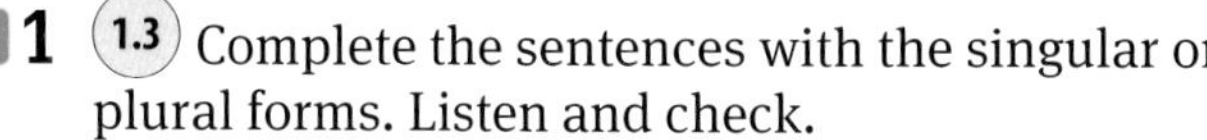

**Nouns:** a bag, a (white)board, a cat, a CD-ROM, a chair, a computer, desks, a door, keys, a kiss, a magazine, a newspaper, a notebook, a noticeboard, phones, sheets of paper, a table, walls, a window

**Question word:** What?

**Expressions:** I can see … . I don't know. Excuse me, please. What's this? What are these?

p.9

**1** (1.3) Complete the sentences with the singular or plural forms. Listen and check.

1 ________ an excellent Nokia mobile.
a This b That's c These are

2 ________ my fantastic new glasses.
a This is b That is c These are

3 ________ my favourite book!
a This is b That is c These are

4 A: ________ CDs?
a That's b Are those c These are
B: No, ________ DVDs.
a these b they're c this is

5 A: ________ your laptop?
a Is that b Are these c This is
B: No, ________ my new desktop computer.
a that's b this is c it's

6 A: ________ your bag?
a Are those b Is this c This is
B: Yes, ________ . It's Gucci, from New York.
a this is b that is c it is

**2** Complete the speech bubbles with *this*, *that*, *these* or *those* and the verb *be*.

1

2

3

4

**3** Complete these classroom nouns with *a*, *e*, *i*, *o* or *u*.

1 *four bags*
2 a b_ _rd
3 a CD-R_M
4 two ch_ _rs
5 a d_sk
6 the d_ _r
7 a n_t_book
8 a n_tic_bo_rd
9 ten sh_ _ts of p_per
10 a t_bl_
11 a w_ll
12 three w_nd_ws

**4** (1.4) Look at Word Bank 3 on p. 66. Listen, repeat and point to the words you hear.

**5** Listen again and write the words. Then check your spelling in Word Bank 3 on p. 66.

# Where are you from?

## Vocabulary

**Word Bank 4:** Countries and nationalities p. 67

**Noun:** people

**Question word:** Who?

**Expressions:** I'm from (Italy). I'm (Italian). Where (in Italy) are you from? Guess! Really? Congratulations! But

**1** Correct the mistake in each sentence.

1 It's an american hotel.

*It's an American hotel.*

2 It's an Australia city.

_______________

3 It's terrible Italian restaurant.

_______________

4 These are a Chinese computers.

_______________

5 This Leo. He's from Britain.

_______________

**2** Circle the correct option.

1 Are you from *Italy* / *Italian*?

2 David and Victoria Beckham aren't *America* / *American*.

3 Is she *Italy* / *English*?

4 Elton John and Prince Charles are from *Britain* / *British*.

p.10 **3** Complete the sentences.

1 Where _______ you from?

I'm Argentinian. _______ _______ Buenos Aires.

2 _______ in Australia are you _______?

_______ from the capital city, Canberra.

3 _______ _______ from Canada?

Yes, I _______ .

4 _______ _______ from England?

No, _______ _______ . We're Scottish.

**4** 1.5 Read and complete the dialogue with the words. One word is not necessary. Listen, check and repeat.

| too | you | see | this | think | sorry |
|---|---|---|---|---|---|
| is | and | meet | are | from | where |

**Alex:** Hey, Lara!

**Lara:** Hello, Alex. (1)________ (2)________ my friend, Lucy.

**Alex:** Hi, Lucy.

**Lucy:** Nice to (3)________ you, Alex.

**Alex:** Nice to meet you, (4)________. (5)________ (6)________ American, Lucy?

**Lucy:** No, I'm English. (7)________ you?

**Alex:** I'm (8)________ Monterrey, in Mexico. (9)________ in England are you from?

**Lucy:** I'm from Brighton.

**Alex:** Really? I (10)________ Brighton is a fantastic city!

**Lucy:** Thank you.

**Lara:** (11)________, Alex. We're late for class.

**Alex:** OK. (12)________ you! Bye!

**Lara/Lucy:** Goodbye.

**5** Do the crossword.

ACROSS

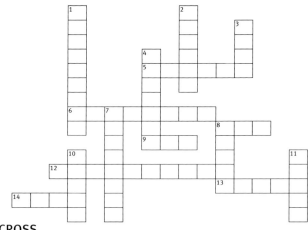

5 Three x four = ...
6 A person from the USA is ...
8 One + one = ...
9 You aren't = You are ...
12 Oporto and Lisbon are ... cities.
13 (Three + one) x two = ...
14 Five + four = ...

DOWN

1 **A:** Are you from Brazil? **B:** Yes, I am. I'm ...
2 Two + nine = ...
3 ... to meet you!
4 Giorgio Armani isn't Spanish. He's ...
7 Cairo, Alexandria and Luxor are ... cities.
8 One, two, ...
10 The Hilton's an excellent ...
11 Matt Damon's an American ...

# I'm a journalist



## Vocabulary

**Word Bank 1:** Numbers 13–29 p. 64 **Nouns:** everybody, a man, a woman
**Word Bank 5:** Jobs, p. 68
**Verbs:** buy cigarettes / alcohol, drive (a car / a moped), work (12) hours a week, can, can't
**Adjectives:** different, divorced, famous, interesting, married, single
**Expressions:** Are you (a/an) ...? No way! What do you do? I'm a(n) .... We're ....
They're .... Wow! That's interesting.

p.12 **1** Circle the correct option.

1 I'm *a secretary / secretary.*
2 We're *a lawyers / lawyers.*
3 I'm *married / a married.*
4 John's *retired / a retired.*
5 They're *a famous actors / famous actors.*
6 You're *excellent students / an excellent students*!

**2** Complete the dialogue.

**Steve:** Hi, I'm Steve. What's your (1) *name* ?
**Maria:** Oh, hello. I'm Maria.
**Steve:** Where (2)______ you (3)______, Maria?
**Maria:** I'm (4)______ Poland.
**Steve:** Poland? That's very interesting. And what do you (5)______, Maria?
**Maria:** (6) I'___ a journalist. I work in London. Oh, Sorry. Steve, (7)______ is Adam.
**Steve:** Hi, Adam. (8)______ you Polish, too?
**Adam:** Yes, I (9)______. I'm (10)______ Warsaw.
**Steve:** And are you and Maria married?
**Maria:** No, we (11)______ . We're divorced.
**Steve:** Oh, sorry.
**Adam:** That's OK. We're good (12)_________ .
**Steve:** And, what (13)______ you (14)______, Adam? (15)______ you a journalist, too?
**Adam:** Me? No! I'm a lawyer, a divorce lawyer.

**3** 1.6 Listen and number the jobs 1–8 in the order you hear them.

| | | |
|---|---|---|
| ☐ an actor | ☐ a housewife | ☐ a doctor |
| ☐ a journalist | ☐ a teacher | ☐ a receptionist |
| ☐ a businessman | ☐ an engineer | ☐ a dentist |
| ☐ a chef | ☐ a writer | ☐ a lawyer |
| ☐ a police officer | ☐ a footballer | ☐ a waiter |

**4** Complete the sentences with jobs from Exercise 3 in the singular or plural forms.

1 Maura Tierney is a *doctor* in the TV drama *ER*.
2 Donald Trump is a successful *b*__________.
3 J.K. Rowling is a British *w*__________.
4 In *Miami Vice*, Sonny Crockett and Ricardo Tubbs are *p*__________ *o*__________.
5 Susan Mayer, Bree Van De Kamp, Gabrielle Solis and Lynette Scavo are the 'Desperate *H*__________'.
6 In *Legally Blonde*, Reese Witherspoon is a *l*__________.

**5** Match the questions and the answers.

1 What do Wayne Rooney and Didier Drogba do?
2 Are Nicole Kidman and Tom Cruise married?
3 Mr Bill Gates, are you a lawyer?
4 Are you and your brother dentists?
5 What do you do?
6 Are you a secretary?
7 Are your friends students?

a ☐ Yes, they're in medical school.
b ☐ Yes, we are. And our father, too!
c ☐ I'm an engineer.
d ☐ No, I'm a receptionist.
e ☐ No, they're divorced.
f [1] They're footballers.
g ☐ No, I'm a businessman.

**6** 1.7 Listen. Circle the numbers you hear. Write the number. Listen again and repeat.

a 14 (40) *forty*
b 80 18 __________
c 19 90 __________
d 50 15 __________
e 17 70 __________
f 16 60 __________

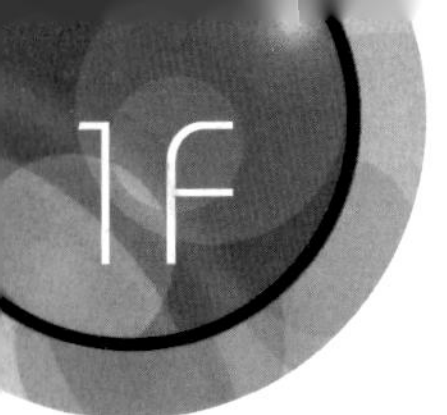


# All about you

## Vocabulary

**Word Bank 1:** High numbers p. 64

**Nouns:** an address, an avenue, home / work phone number, an occupation, a road, a street, a way

## Test yourself on unit 1

1. Do these exercises to check your progress.
2. Count your **correct** answers. Write the total number in the box.

**Total:** ☐ /39 correct answers

3. Try to understand your mistakes. If necessary,
   - read the **Essential Grammar**, and/or
   - look at the Student Book lesson again, or
   - ask your teacher.
4. How do you feel about this unit? Tick (✓) a box.

☐ ☐ ☐ ☐ ☐

*I can ... ask for and give personal information.* Lesson 1F

**1** Bob's at a job interview. Look at his answers and write the interviewer's questions.

1 Bob Davies.
2 I'm from the USA.
3 I'm an actor, but I'm unemployed at the moment.
4 No, I'm single.
5 077 5123 6578
6 It's 279, High Road, London.


1 *What's your name?*
2 ______
3 ______
4 ______
5 ______
6 ______

*I can ... give my opinion, using articles and adjectives correctly.* Lessons 1A–1B

**2** Tick (✓) the correct sentences. Correct the wrong sentences.

1 They're terrible English students. ☐
______
2 Berlin's a city fantastic in Germany. ☐
______
3 Al Pacino's a actor excellent. ☐
______
4 *The Da Vinci Code*'s a famous book. ☐
______
5 Lionel Messi's a footballer Argentinian. ☐
______

*I can ... introduce myself.* Lessons 1A–1B

**3** Complete the words in the dialogue.

**Day 1 in an English class.**

**Student:** (1) *G*______ evening. (2) *A*______ (3) *y*______ John Smith, the English teacher?

**Teacher:** Yes, I (4) *a*______. And you? (5) *A*______ (6) *y*______ Katia Putin?

**Student:** No, I'm (7) *n*______, sorry. (8) *I*______ Linda Lee.

**Teacher:** Come in, Linda. (9) *N*______ (10) *t*______ (11) *m*______ (12) *y*______ .

*I can ... identify and name objects and people.* Lesson 1C

**4** Write the sentences in the plural.

1 What's this? Is it a hairbrush?
*What are these? Are they hairbrushes?*

2 That's a BMW. It's an excellent car.
______________________

3 This is a Montblanc pen. Is it good?
______________________

4 This isn't a Swiss watch. It's a Nike watch.
______________________

5 Is that newspaper in English?
______________________

**5** Complete the sentences with *this*, *that*, *these* or *those*.

1 '________ coffee is wonderful! It's from Colombia.'

2 '________ are terrible restaurants.'

3 'Are ________ books in English?'

4 '________ is Dick Anderson. He's a famous lawyer.'

*I can ... talk about nationalities and countries.* Lesson 1D

**6** Write the sentences.

| | | | |
|---|---|---|---|
| 1 | Turkey | I'm *Turkish*. | *I'm from Turkey*. |
| 2 | the USA | We ________. | We ________. |
| 3 | China | They ________. | They ________. |
| 4 | Spain | ____ you ________? | ____ you ________? |
| 5 | Germany | I ________. | ________. |

*I can ... ask and answer about jobs.* Lesson 1E

**7** Match the questions and answers. One answer is not necessary.

1 Are you an engineer?
2 What do you do, Karin?
3 Are you and Sally chefs?
4 Are David and Mike police officers?
5 What do you do, Ana? And you, Tim?

a ☐ We're journalists.
b ☐ No, we aren't. We're civil servants.
c ☐ No, they aren't. They're unemployed at the moment.
d ☑ *1* Yes, I am.
e ☐ No, I'm not. I'm an engineer.
f ☐ I'm a dentist.

*Now I can ... say 250 words in English.* Lessons 1A–1F

**8** Cover the words and test yourself on ...

1 WB Numbers 1 to 10,000,000 (p. 64).
Can you say the 44 numbers?

2 WB Classroom instructions (p. 65).
Can you remember the 8 expressions?

3 The classroom (p. 8).
Can you remember the 12 things in the photo?

4 WB Personal things (p. 66).
Can you remember the 20 things?

5 WB Countries and nationalities (p. 67).
Can you pronounce the 30 countries and nationalities with the correct stress?

6 WB Jobs (p. 68).
Can you remember the 20 jobs?

7 Phrasebook 1 (p. 77) Look only at your translations.
Can you say the phrases in English?

# 2A In Paris on Thursday

## Vocabulary

**Word Bank 6A:** The alphabet p. 69
**Nouns:** beer, coffee, drink (verb and noun), ice, milk, mineral water, orange juice, sugar, tea, wine
**Adjectives:** favourite, happy **Other:** very
**Days of the week:** Sunday, Monday, Tuesday, Wednesday, Thursday, Friday, Saturday
**Prepositions:** from (Monday) to (Friday), on (Saturday)
**Expressions:** How do you spell ...? Is that right? Yes, you're right. No problem.
Sorry, you're wrong. Let's go. Where are they on ...? Are they in ... on ...?
Would you like a ...?

**1** (2.1) Listen and repeat. Circle the letter with a different sound.

| | | | | |
|---|---|---|---|---|
| 1 | A | H | (G) | K |
| 2 | B | C | D | F |
| 3 | E | J | P | T |
| 4 | I | L | M | N |
| 5 | Q | U | V | W |
| 6 | X | Y | Z | S |

p.18 **2** Circle the correct verb and complete the sentences with *in* or *on*.

1 Pedro and Carla *am / is / (are)* _in_ Warsaw _on_ Tuesday.
2 Dublin *am / is / are* a beautiful city ___ Ireland.
3 Where *am / is / are* you ___ Wednesday?
4 I *am / is / are* ___ Hamburg ___ Sunday.
5 They *am / is / are* ___ Paris ___ Monday evening.

**3** Put the words in the correct order.

1 are / where / Tuesday / on / they / ?
______________________
2 Sammy and Kate / on / are / Thursday / Moscow / in / ?
______________________
3 evening / are / Brussels / they / in / on / Sunday /?
______________________
4 Friday / 're / on / we / in / Beijing
______________________
5 Prague / they / aren't / on / afternoon / in / Wednesday
______________________
6 in / on / Thailand / I / evening / 'm / Friday
______________________

**4** Complete the e-mail with *in* or *on*.

From: *Let's Go* agency
To: Zack and Tom
Subject: South American adventure holiday

Dear Zack and Tom

Here's your South American adventure holiday programme:

You're (1) _on_ flight AA738 (2)_____ Monday morning from JFK airport to Simón Bolívar airport (3)_____ Caracas. (4)_____ Tuesday you're (5)_____ Venezuela and (6)_____ Wednesday afternoon, you're (7)_____ Peru to visit beautiful Machu Picchu. Then, you're skiing (8)_____ Chile (9) _____ Friday and Saturday. Finally, your flight from Santiago to Los Angeles is AA4414 (10) _____ Sunday morning.

Have a fantastic holiday!
Robert Crowe

**5** Read the e-mail again. Write T (true) or F (false).

1 They're in Venezuela on Tuesday. ___
2 They're in Peru on Friday. ___
3 They're in Chile on Saturday. ___
4 They're in Chile on Sunday afternoon. ___

**6** (2.2) Complete the dialogue with the words. Listen and check.

thank yes you coffee very here
welcome ~~madam~~ are orange juice no

**Attendant:** Would you like a drink, (1) _madam_?
**Mrs Caldwell:** Yes. (2)_________ _________, please.
**Attendant:** Ice?
**Mrs Caldwell:** (3)_________, please.
**Attendant:** (4)_________ you are, madam.
**Mrs Caldwell:** (5)_________ you.
**Attendant:** You're (6)_________. And for (7)_____, sir?
**Mr Caldwell:** (8)_________ for me, please.
**Attendant:** Sugar?
**Mr Caldwell:** (9)_____, thanks.
**Attendant:** Here you (10)_____.
**Mr Caldwell:** Thank you (11)_____ much.

# How old is he?

2B

## Vocabulary

**Nouns:** an artist, a celebrity, a charity, chocolate, a company, a dancer, a film star, a model, the president, a quiz, a singer, a TV presenter, the winner, a writer

**Adjective:** important

**Expressions:** I'm not sure. How old (is he)? (He's) about (20) years old. Who's this?

**1** Match the questions and answers.

1 Who's this man in the photo?
2 Is this car a Ferrari?
3 Is Amsterdam the capital of Holland?
4 What this in English?
5 Is Paris Hilton French?
6 How old is Paris? Is she 22?
7 Where's her father Richard Hilton from?

a ☐ No, it isn't. It's The Hague.
b ☐ It's a lipstick.
c [1] That's Li. He's my Korean friend.
d ☐ No, no way. She's about 28.
e ☐ No, it isn't. It's a Mercedes.
f ☐ No, she's American, from New York, I think.
g ☐ He's American, too, from California.

21 **2** Complete the dialogues with *is*, *'s*, *isn't*, *where* or *how old*.

1 **A:** _How_ _old's_ Bob?
**B:** I think he _______ about 45 years old.
2 **A:** _______ Cameron Diaz from New Zealand?
**B:** No, she _______. She _______ American.
3 **A:** _______ is the tango from?
**B:** It _______ from Argentina.
4 **A:** _______ _______ the Parthenon in Athens?
**B:** It _______ about 2,500 years old.

**3** Correct one mistake in each sentence.

1 Is he of Berlin?
_Is he from Berlin?_
2 He's about 50 year old.
_______________
3 How old your mother's?
_______________
4 She isn't singer.
_______________
5 My teachers's 24 years.
_______________

**4** Complete the questions with *is* or *are*. Write short answers with the correct pronoun.

1 _Is_ Johnny Depp married? _No, he isn't._
2 _______ Pedro Almodóvar a Spanish film director? Yes, _______.
3 _______ you a civil servant? _______
4 _______ David Beckham and Victoria married? Yes, _______.
5 _______ the Colosseum in Rome about 1,000 years old? No, _______. It's 2,000 years old.
6 _______ the Mayan city of Chichen Itza in Mexico? Yes, _______ .

**5** (2.3) Read the text and circle the correct option. Listen and check.

Johnny Depp's a famous [1]*chef / singer / actor*. He lives [2]*at / on / in* France, but he [3]*aren't / 'm not / isn't* French. He's [4]*English / the USA / American*, from Kentucky. He [5]*'s / 're / 'm* in many films, including *Pirates of the Carribean* and [6]*are / is / am* a Golden Globe winner. And he [7]*'s / 're / 'm* about 47 years old! I think he [8]*'re / 's / 'm* fantastic!

### Study tip

**Remember phrases not just words**

1 Remember words in phrases, not single words. For example, *Sorry, I'm late. That's OK. Just a moment, please. Nice to meet you.*
2 Write new words in phrases in your vocabulary notebook. For example, not just the word 'rubber', but 'a rubber', or 'Can I use your rubber, please?'
3 Write a translation in pencil. Test yourself to memorise the phrases.
4 Use the phrases when you can in class.

# 2C His music, her show, their charities

## Vocabulary

**Nouns:** a child / children, an electric guitar, e-mail address, a fan, a fax, a hometown, a racing car, a shirt, a twin sister, a website, a wife

**Possessive adjectives:** my, your, his, her, their **Other:** now

**Expressions:** This is correct. What's (his) e-mail?

p.22 **1** Put in the missing *'s*.

1 My favourite black and white film's *Schindler's List.*
2 It's one of Steven Spielberg films.
3 My favourite jeans are Levi.
4 My favourite CD's Elton John Greatest Hits.
5 I love the burgers at McDonald.
6 'To be or not to be, that is the question' says Hamlet in Shakespeare famous play.

**2** Complete the video club form.

★★★★★ **FIVE-STAR VIDEO CLUB** ★★★★★

**Membership Form**

(1)Name: ______

(2)Surname: ______

(3)Address: ______

(4)E-mail: ______

(5)Phone no: ______

(6)Age: ______

(7)Occupation: ______

(8)Nationality: ______

p.23 **3** Complete the sentences with *his*, *her* or *their*.

1 That's *Jamie Oliver's* restaurant.
That's _his_ restaurant.
2 David Beckham's *parents* love Manchester United.
It's ______ favourite football team.
3 That's *Avril Lavigne's* guitar.
It's ______ guitar.
4 That's *Lewis Hamilton's* racing car.
It's ______ racing car.
5 That's *my teacher's* memory stick.
It's ______ memory stick.

**4** Complete the sentences with *my*, *your*, *his*, *her* or *their*.

1 He's a good artist. ______ name's Don Owen.
2 I'm 42 years old, ______ brother is 44, my sister is 47 and ______ mother is 68.
3 **Laura:** What's ______ mobile phone number?
**Larry:** It's 077856 3548. Please phone me.
4 Paul and Lucy are married. ______ address is 344 Fulham Road, London.
5 Linda Gibson is the company president.
______ e-mail is lgibson65@ig.com.

**5** Read the text. Circle the correct word / pronoun to substitute the underlined names.

Susan Sarandon is a famous actress, model and film producer from New York. (1)Susan's partner is Tim Robbins, who is a famous American actor, too. One of (2)Tim Robbins' famous films is *The Player*. (3)Susan and Tim live in New York City with (4)Susan and Tim's children, Jack Henry and Miles Guthrie. *Thelma and Louise* is one of (5)Susan's films. (6)Susan and Tim aren't married. The difference in (7)Susan and Tim's age is 12 years, but (8)Susan and Tim are very happy together.

| | a | b | c | d |
|---|---|---|---|---|
| 1 | She | (Her) | His | Your |
| 2 | he | her | his | your |
| 3 | Their | His | You | They |
| 4 | they | his | their | your |
| 5 | she | his | her | their |
| 6 | We | Their | Your | They |
| 7 | their | your | you | his |
| 8 | their | they | you | we're |

# Do you have a big family?

## Vocabulary

**Word Bank 7:** Your family p. 70

**Nouns:** a city, a motorbike, a partner, a town, a village **Verbs:** have, live

**Adjectives:** big, small, dead, alive

**Expressions:** How nice! I only have ... . Oh, really? Oh, I see. **Adverb:** alone

**1** (2.4) Write sentences about the family using *'s*. Listen and check.

Ronald — Nancy

Mary — Paul Rebecca Lisa — Richard

Peter Shirley

1 Nancy – Ronald

*Nancy is Ronald's wife.*

2 Lisa – Paul

____________________

3 Peter and Shirley – Ronald

____________________

4 Shirley – Lisa and Richard

____________________

5 Richard – Rebecca

____________________

6 Ronald and Nancy – Lisa

____________________

7 Rebecca – Richard

____________________

8 Ronald – Shirley

____________________

25 **2** Complete the dialogues with *do*, *don't*, *have* or *live*.

1 **A:** _____ you _____ in a flat?

**B:** Yes, I _____. It's big and it's in a very nice street.

2 **A:** _____ Cindy and Gary _____ children?

**B:** No, they _____. But they _____ three dogs and a cat.

3 **A:** Hi. I'm at the market. _____ we _____ milk and sugar for breakfast?

**B:** Yes, we _____. Oh, but we _____ _____ orange juice.

4 **A:** _____ you _____ a big family?

**B:** Yes, I _____. I _____ my parents, two brothers and one sister.

**3** Make the sentences negative.

1 I have a British grandfather.

*I don't have a British grandfather.*

2 We live alone.

____________________

3 Joe and I have a big family.

____________________

4 They live with their parents.

____________________

**4** Write full questions. Every ✻ = one missing word.

1 ✻ you live ✻ ✻ parents?

*Do you live with your parents?*

2 ✻ you have children?

____________________?

3 ✻ your children have English classes ✻ Tuesday?

____________________?

4 ✻ you live ✻ ✻ flat?

____________________?

5 ✻ Lee and Jo live ✻ India ✻ their parents?

____________________?

**5** Read the e-mail. Find and circle 10 mistakes. Correct the mistakes.

| | | |
|---|---|---|
| | | Dear Jeff |
| 1 | *name's* | My name Marek and I'm in your class |
| 2 | _____ | in Tuesday and Thursday evenings. |
| 3 | _____ | I'm from Polish. My phone |
| 4 | _____ | number 0778655120. I'm not married |
| 5 | _____ | but I have partner. |
| 6 | _____ | We together in a flat here |
| 7 | _____ | on Birmingham. |
| 8 | _____ | His name's Mary and |
| 9 | _____ | she's teacher, too. |
| | | I love your classes and I think |
| 10 | _____ | you're a teacher great. |
| | | Best wishes, |
| | | Marek |

# Meet your perfect partner

## Vocabulary

**Word Bank 4:** Languages p. 67

**Nouns:** languages, a shop, sports (volleyball, football, tennis)

**Adjectives:** important, perfect, successful

**Verbs:** ask

**Adverbs:** a lot, a little, (not) very well

**Expressions:** Call me. Great! It's a terrible habit. I work for (a company). I work in (a shop). Very important

p.27 **1** Put the words in the correct order.

1 speak / well / do / German / you ?

*Do you* ______________________

2 sports / play / do / well / what / you ?

______________________

3 do / lot / you / smoke / a ?

______________________

4 work / do / parents / where / your ?

______________________

5 have / children / you / do / how / many ?

______________________

6 do / speak / well / languages / what / you ?

______________________

**2** Complete what they say. Use the words in the box.

| ~~like~~ play smoke speak a well little ~~lot~~ |
|---|

**A** *I like my job a lot!*

**B** *We ________ football very ________!*

**C** *Bonjour! I ________ a ________ French.*

**D** *I ________ ________ lot. It's a terrible habit!*

STOP SMOKING

**3** Match the incomplete dialogues 1–4 and people A–D in Exercise 2.

1 **A:** ________ you smoke?
**B:** Yes, ________ ________. Thirty cigarettes a day.

2 **A:** ________ ________ do you ________?
**B:** English, Spanish and a ________ French.

3 **A:** ________ your children ________ football?
**B:** Yes, they love it. And they play it ________, too. They're excellent football players.

4 **A:** ________ do you ________?
**B:** In the city centre, for a big computer company.

**4** Complete the dialogues in Exercise 3 with the words.

| little what languages work do (x3) where speak I play well |
|---|

**5** (2.5) Listen to Jane's profile. Write T (true) or F (false).

1 Jane's 30 years old. ___
2 Jane lives in England. ___
3 Jane's perfect man is about 35 years old. ___
4 Jane's perfect man is Spanish. ___
5 Jane's perfect man likes children a lot. ___

**6** Imagine you're Larry Roberts, Jane's 'perfect' man. Complete the text.

*I'm perfect for Jane. I (1) ________ 32 and I like (2) ________ a lot. I (3) ________ smoke or (4) ________ football. I work for an international bank and I (5) ________ a Mercedes. Oh, and I speak Spanish (6) ________ (7) ________.*

# What do you do at the weekend?

## Vocabulary

**Word Bank 8:** Free time p. 71

**Nouns:** a bike, the city centre, a dog, soft drinks, a flat / an apartment, a goldfish, a pet, a soap opera

**Prepositions:** in (a flat), in (the morning), at (the weekend), (on) Friday morning

**Adverb:** usually

**Expressions:** I see. What do you do (on Saturday morning)? Me, too.

## Test yourself on unit 2

1. Do these exercises to check your progress.
2. Count your **correct** answers. Write the total number in the box.

**Total:** ☐ /42 correct answers

3. Try to understand your mistakes. If necessary,
   - read the **Essential Grammar**, and/or
   - look at the Student Book lesson again, or
   - ask your teacher.
4. How do you feel about this unit? Tick (✓) a box.

☐ ☐ ☐ ☐ ☐

*I can ... ask for and give new information.* Lesson 2F

**1** Read Jane's answers and write Larry's questions.

1 **Larry:** ____________________?

**Jane:** In a small flat in Sydney.

2 **Larry:** ____________________?

**Jane:** I work for Smith & Sons. It's a small law office.

3 **Larry:** ____________________?

**Jane:** It's in the city centre, in King Street.

4 **Larry:** ____________________?

**Jane:** I usually go out with friends on Saturdays and relax on Sundays.

*I can ... talk about free-time activities.* Lesson 2F

**2** Complete the sentences with the correct free-time activity and circle the correct preposition.

1 I usually stay at home *at* / *(on)* / *in* Friday morning.

2 My brother and I *sp*_________ time *on*_________ *at* / *in* / *on* the afternoon.

3 *On* / *At* / *In* the weekend I usually go *sh*_________ with my *f*_________.

4 *On* / *At* / *In* Sunday evening my parents _________ TV. They love watching good films.

5 *On* / *At* / *In* Saturday I *r*_________ a book or *l*_________ to *m*_________.

*I can ... say where and when with the correct prepositions.* Lesson 2A

**3** Complete the sentences with *on* or *in*.

1 I study English ____ Mondays and Wednesdays.

2 The Giza Pyramids are ____ Cairo, ____ Egypt.

3 **A:** Tell me about your holiday programme, Marco. Where are you ____ Friday evening?

**B:** I'm ____ France, ____ Paris, at the Eiffel Tower with my girlfriend.

*I can ... ask for a drink.* Lesson 2B

**4** Put the dialogue in the correct order.

**Attendant:**

☐ Sugar?

☐ Here you are, sir.

[1] Would you like a drink, sir?

☐ You're welcome.

☐ Milk?

**Mr Wilde:**

☐ Yes. Tea, please.

[4] No, thanks. No sugar today!

☐ Yes, please. A lot!

☐ Thank you very much.

*I can ... ask for and give information about people / things.* Lesson 2B

**5** Make questions. Each ✻ = one missing word.

1 ✻ Bob Dylan ✻ famous American singer?

______________________________

2 Where ✻ Nicole Kidman from?

______________________________

3 How old ✻ Fidel Castro?

______________________________

4 ✻ *100 Years of Solitude* ✻ good book?

______________________________

5 ✻ *Casablanca* ✻ French film?

______________________________

**6** Match the questions in Exercise 5 and the correct answers. There is one extra answer.

a ☐ No, it isn't. It's from the USA.
b ☐ She's from Australia.
c ☐ Yes, it is. It's brilliant.
d ☐ No, it isn't. It's American. It's a fantastic film.
e ☐ Yes, he is. He's very popular.
f ☐ I think he's about 80.

*I can ... talk about people's possessions.* Lesson 2C

**7** Write *my*, *your*, *his*, *her* or *their*.

*1 'Is this ______ pen?'*

*2 'That's Pedro – and that's ______ girlfriend, Elena!'*

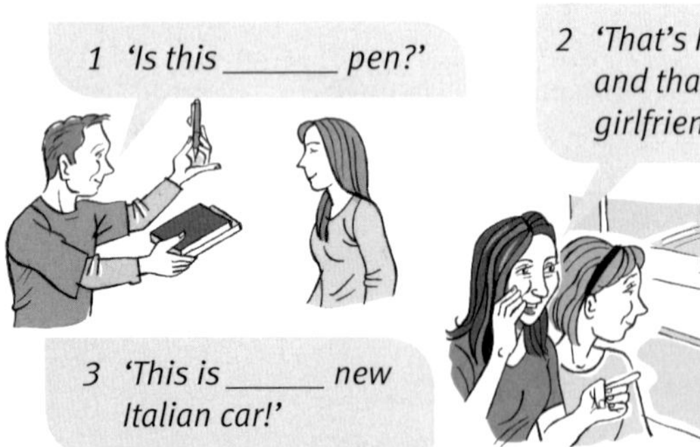

*3 'This is ______ new Italian car!'*

*4 'That's Victoria. ______ husband is a famous footballer.'*

*5 '______ family is fantastic!'*

*I can ... talk about families.* Lesson 2D

**8** Make questions with *have* or *live*. Write short answers.

1 you – alone? ✓

*Do you live alone? Yes, I do.*

2 you and your family – a car? ✗

______________________________

3 David and Sue – children? ✓

______________________________.

4 you – with your parents? ✗

______________________________.

*I can ... ask for and give every day information.* Lesson 2E

**9** Write sentences about Hugh and Linda.

Do you ...?

| | |
|---|---|
| 1 have a car? | Yes, we do. |
| 2 like children? | Yes, a lot. |
| 3 play football? | No, we don't. |
| 4 Where do you work? | In a big company in Boston. |
| 5 What sports do you play? | Handball and tennis. |

1 *Hugh and Linda have a car.*
2 Hugh and Linda ______________________.
3 They ______________________.
4 They ______________________.
5 ______________________

*I can ... spell and say 150 more words in English* Lessons 2A–2F

**10** Cover the words and test yourself on ...

1 WB The alphabet (p. 69) Can you pronounce the 26 letters?
2 WB Your family (p. 70) Can you pronounce the 13 words with the correct stress?
3 WB Free time (p. 71) Can you remember the 17 verb phrases?
4 WB Languages (p. 67) Can you pronounce the 12 different languages with the correct stress?
5 Phrasebook 2 (p. 77) Look at your translations. Can you say the phrases in English?

# Let's watch a DVD tonight



## Vocabulary

**Word Bank 9:** Adjectives p. 72

**Nouns:** a request, a suggestion

**Expressions:** Can I have ...? Can you lend me ...? Can you open the door, please?
Can I use ...? Let's go out tonight. Of course. Sorry, I can't. Sure.
OK, why not? That's a good idea. Right, then. It's an emergency.

**1** Match the requests and the pictures, A–D.

1 ☐ Can you close that window, please? It's cold!
2 ☐ Can you stop that, please? I can't think!
3 ☐ Excuse me, can you open the door, please?
4 ☐ Help! Can I use your phone please? It's an emergency!

**2** Complete the sentences with *Can I*, *Can you* or *Let's*. Use the question marks (?) to help you.

1 ________ go to a restaurant.
2 ________ open the door for me, please?
3 ________ watch a football match.
4 ________ use your mobile?
5 ________ play cards tonight.
6 ________ see your holiday photos?
7 ________ go out for a moment, please?
8 ________ help me, please?
9 ________ do exercise 2!

**3** Are 1–8 suggestions or requests? Write *S* or *R*.

1 Let's go to the park to play football. [S]
2 Let's go to the *Coldplay* concert! ☐
3 Can I borrow your pen, please? ☐
4 Let's chat online tonight. ☐
5 I'm hungry! Let's go to Ali Baba's. ☐
6 Can I speak to Mona, please? ☐
7 Let's go shopping. ☐
8 Can I have a beer, please? ☐

**4** Match 1–8 in Exercise 3, and the answers, a–h.

a [4] Sure. On Skype or MSN?
b ☐ Sorry, she isn't home now.
c ☐ That's a good idea. I love their music!
d ☐ Sorry, I don't have any money.
e ☐ OK. Blue or black?
f ☐ Sorry, we don't serve alcohol.
g ☐ Sorry, we can't. We don't have a ball.
h ☐ Great idea! I love Egyptian food!

**5** (3.1) Listen and complete the dialogues.

1 **A:** Voulez-vous un café, monsieur?
**B:** *Can you* speak slowly, please? I'm Australian.

2 **A:** ______ ______ use my American Express card?
**B:** ______, I'm ______ . We ______ take credit cards.

3 **A:** ______ ______ have a Diet Coke, please?
**B:** ______, here you ______ .

4 **A:** ______ go to the Ritz Hotel for a ______ .
**B:** Er, no, I ______ think that's a good ______!

**6** (3.2) What's the problem? Listen and match person, 1–3, to a sentence, A–C.

A ☐ I'm really bored.
B ☐ I'm really ill.
C ☐ I'm really busy.

# Ordinary people?

## Vocabulary

**Nouns:** a biography, jeans, a leader, a liquid, Physics, the Queen, a scientist, the sea, a spider, a suit, a university, the weather

**Adjectives:** extraordinary, fast, ordinary, long (hair), strong, typical

**Verbs:** change into (a superhero), come from (Britain), fly, jump, run (up walls), wear, work as (a photographer)

**Expressions:** It's the same in my language. For example, ...

p.34 **1** Read Victoria Beckham. Write sentences about her. Do you think she's ordinary or extraordinary?

1 go skiing a lot ✓
2 have three children ✓
3 live in Los Angeles ✓
4 drink a lot of green tea ✓
5 like meat ✗
6 read books or newspapers ✗
7 listen to music a lot ✓
8 play football ✗

1 *Victoria goes skiing a lot.*
2 *She* ________.
3 *She* ________.
4 ________
5 ________
6 ________
7 ________
8 ________

**2** (3.3) Complete the text with the verbs in the Present simple. Who is he? Listen and check.

work  live  ~~come~~  not have  fly  use  wear (×2)

### Biography 3

This extraordinary man (1) *comes* from the Planet Krypton, but now he (2) ________ in the city of Metropolis. He (3) ________ the name Clark Kent. He (4) ________ for a newspaper, the *Daily Planet*. He (5) ________ glasses. He's married and his wife, Lois Lane, is a reporter, too but he (6) ________ any children. He's really, really strong and he (7) ________ very, very fast. He (8) ________ a special red and blue suit and his Superhero name is ...

**3** Make true sentences with the verbs, positive or negative.

1 The Queen of England ________ in a flat. (live)
2 Tiger Woods ________ basketball. (play)
3 My English teacher ________ in an office. (work)
4 My teacher ________ from England. (come)
5 My mobile ________ a video camera in it. (have)
6 My sister ________ at university. (study)
7 My best friend ________ as a chef. (work)
8 My mother ________ glasses. (wear)

**4** Complete the sentences with the verbs.

smoke  like  ~~love~~  drink  speak

1 That's a great car! My wife *loves* it, too.
2 Rod and Fiona really don't like cigarettes. They ________ .
3 Kate's a good translator. She ________ German, Spanish and French very well.
4 I ________ jazz. It's terrible!
5 Li ________ orange juice every day. It's her favourite.

**5** (3.4) Listen. Write T (true) or F (false). Correct the false sentences.

1 Anna's husband is a lawyer. F
*Anna's husband is a writer.*
2 Her husband likes coffee very much. ___
________
3 Paolo doesn't play football or watch it on TV. ___
________
4 Kate doesn't think Paolo's a typical Italian. ___
________
5 Paolo doesn't like Italian food. ___
________
6 Anna wants to go to a Chinese restaurant. ___
________

# Does he like you? Yes, he does!

3C

## Vocabulary

**Nouns:** animals **Adjectives:** intelligent, lovely, personal (life)
**Verbs:** dance, do exercise, eat meat, sing, support (a team)
**Expressions:** Well, ... I (don't) think so.

3.7 **1** Circle the correct form.

1 My car doesn't *has* / *have* a DVD player.

2 Shrek *doesn't love* / *loves* Cinderella. He *love* / *loves* Fiona.

3 **A:** *Do* / *Does* Shakira speak English well?
**B:** Of course she *do* / *does*. She *sing* / *sings* in English and *do* / *does* interviews in English, too.

4 **A:** Does Madonna *live* / *lives* in the USA?
**B:** No, she *don't* / *doesn't*. She *live* / *lives* in Britain. She *has* / *have* houses in London and Scotland.
**A:** She's very strong. *Do* / *Does* she go to the gym?
**B:** Yes, she *do* / *does*. For two or three hours every day.
**A:** What about food? *Do* / *Does* she eat meat?
**B:** No, she *don't* / *doesn't*. And she *don't* / *doesn't* drink alcohol.

**2** Complete the sentences with *does* or *doesn't*.

1 **A:** __________ George Bush speak French?
**B:** No, he __________. But, he speaks Spanish I think and English, of course.

2 **A:** And, __________ he have any brothers?
**B:** Yes, he __________. He has three brothers.

3 **A:** What about children? ________ he have kids?
**B:** Yes, he ________. He has twin daughters.

4 **A:** Finally, __________ he play football or basketball?
**B:** No, he __________, but he plays tennis.

**3** Make 1–3 negative and 4–6 questions.

1 She likes football.
*She doesn't like football.*

2 My wife and I speak Japanese.
__________________________________

3 Henry sings in Mandarin Chinese.
__________________________________

4 You smoke a lot.
*Do you smoke a lot?*

5 Susan has a very good job.
__________________________________

6 David's friends watch TV a lot.
__________________________________

**4** Read about Naomi Bale. Complete sentences 1–9 with the verbs, positive or negative.

My name's Naomi Bale. I'm 29 years old and I live in Toronto, in a small flat. I speak English, French and Italian. I'm an engineer and I work for a big Canadian company in the city centre. I love Mexican food, especially tacos! I don't drink beer or wine, but I drink a lot of water. I have a small dog, Mimi. She's my best friend!

In the evening, I watch TV or listen to music. I like all types of music. At the weekend, I do a lot of exercise and I spend time with my friends. We usually meet on Saturday afternoons and we go out all night! On Sundays, I go for a walk with my partner, and we have a barbecue at home or go to a restaurant for lunch. In the evening, we usually go to the cinema. We really love good films.

1 Naomi *doesn't speak* four languages. (speak)
2 She __________ a secretary. (be)
3 She __________ for an American company. (work)
4 She __________ Mexican food a lot. (like)
5 She __________ a dog. (have)
6 She __________ to music in the evening. (listen)
7 She __________ a lot of exercise. (do)
8 She __________ to the cinema on Saturday night. (go)
9 She __________ bad films. (like)

**5** 3.5 Race the CD! Listen and answer 10 questions about Naomi before the BEEP! Use *Yes, she does* or *No, she doesn't*. Correct the wrong information.

*Does she live in England? No, she doesn't. She lives in Canada.*

# Look at the time!

## Vocabulary

**Word Bank 10:** The time p. 73

**Question word:** When?

**Prepositions:** at 6.15 p.m. / on MTV

**Expressions:** What channel / time is it on? When's it on?

**Noun:** a TV guide, the news

**Verbs:** start, end

**1** 3.6 Complete the times. Listen, check and repeat.

1 7:00 It's seven ________.

2 4:10 It's four ________.

3 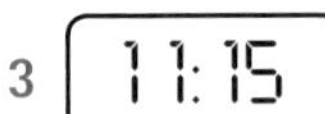

It's ________ fifteen.

4 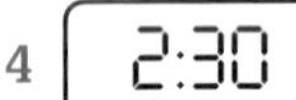

It's two ________.

5 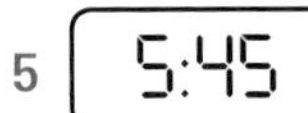

It's ________ forty-five.

6 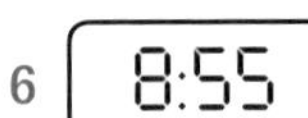

It's eight ________.

**2** Write the times. Use the 'other system'.

What time is it?

1 *It's half past three.*

2 ________

3 ________

4 ________

5 ________

6 ________

p.39 **3** Complete the dialogue.

**A:** Let's watch *Match of the Day*.

**B:** Sure. What time's it (1)________?

**A:** I'm not sure, but I know it's (2)________ Saturday evenings.

**B:** What time (3)________ it start? Can you look in the TV guide?

**A:** OK. Er, it (4)________ (5)________ 10.30. What time (6)________ it now?

**B:** (7)________'s 11.30!

**A:** It can't be 11.30.

**B:** It is! What (8)________ does *Match of the Day* (9)________?

**A:** It ends (10)________ midnight.

**B:** Well, we can see some of the games. Come on. Let's go home.

**A:** OK! Let's run!

**4** 3.7 Listen to Martha talk about her typical day. Number the activities in order, 1–13.

- [ ] go to bed ____
- [ ] have a shower ____
- [I] get up ____
- [ ] watch the news ____
- [ ] do exercise ____
- [ ] go home ____
- [ ] drive children to school ____
- [ ] go to work
- [ ] have breakfast
- [II] have dinner
- [ ] have lunch
- [ ] go online
- [ ] do homework

**5** Listen again. Write the times Martha says next to the *seven* verbs in the left column.

# What time do you get up?

## Vocabulary

**Word Bank 11:** Everyday activities p. 74
**Nouns:** bacon, eggs, sausages, a comedy, a person, the radio, (film) review, the theatre
**Adjectives:** another, different (to), horrible, romantic, similar (to), social (life), successful
**Adverb:** exactly **Prepositions:** before, after
**Expressions:** Don't miss it!

**1** (3.8) Listen and order the activities, 1–6.

a ☐ get up  d ☐ finish school
b ☐ do exercise  e ☐ get home
c ☐ have shower  f ☐ go to bed

p.41 **2** Complete the dialogues. Circle the correct option.

1 A: ________ ________ Jack Nicholson do?
B: ________ *make / makes* films. He's a famous actor.

2 A: Where ________ Jack *live / lives*?
B: He *live / lives* ________ a big house in Hollywood.

3 A: ________ *do / does* the manager *finish / finishes* work?
B: He *finish / finishes* work at about six o'clock.

4 A: ________ *do / does* your partner *work / works*?
B: She *work / works* in a theatre company. She's an actress.

5 A: ________ *do / does* your best friend usually *do / does* in the morning?
B: She usually *study / studies* a little and then *go / goes* to university.

**3** Put the words in the correct order.

1 what time / you / breakfast / do / have ?
*What time do you have breakfast?*

2 your / work / best / where / friend / does ?
________________

3 Sunday / up / I / on / before / don't / get / 11.00 a.m.
________________

4 does / mother / instrument / play / what / your ?
________________

5 home / do / get / what time / from / you / school ?
________________

6 family / where / your / holiday / on / does / go ?
________________

**4** Answer these questions.

1 What time is it now?
________________

2 What time does your favourite TV programme start?
________________

3 What time do you usually go to bed?
________________

4 Where does your best friend work?
________________

5 What do you usually have for lunch?
________________

**5** Read the text and circle the correct option.

Nathan Smith's from Birmingham, England and he's a busy man. He usually (1)____ up (2)____ 7 a.m. and has orange juice, sausages and bread (3)____ breakfast. After that, he (4)____ a shower and then (5)____ home. He's a civil servant and (6)____ in a big office. He (7)____ work at 9 a.m. and usually (8)____ very late, after 7 p.m. After work he's usually very (9)____ . He (10)____ home at about 8 and (11)____ his dinner. He (12)____ to bed at 10 p.m.

1 a get  b (gets)
2 a on  b at
3 a for  b of
4 a has  b have
5 a arrives  b leaves
6 a lives  b works
7 a finishes  b starts
8 a finishes  b starts
9 a tired  b bored
10 a gets  b leaves
11 a makes  b don't eat
12 a comes  b goes

**6** (3.9) Listen and check.

**Study tip**

**Listen every day!**

1 To learn English fast, it's really important to listen to English every day. For example, listen to your Student's CD, the TV (with subtitles in your language), songs in English, the Internet, etc.

2 Listen for five minutes every day. It can help you to understand, to speak and to pronounce well.

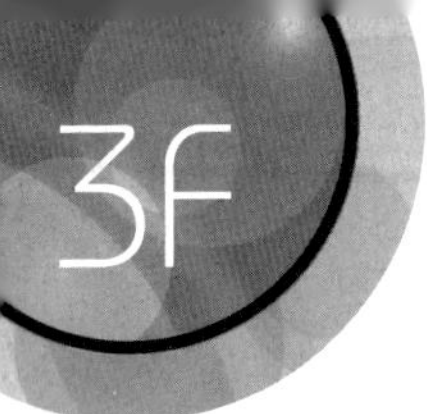

# He always leaves home early

## Vocabulary

**Nouns:** a cookbook, food, a reality show
**Verbs:** ask (somebody) to, make (a reservation), need, phone
**Adjective:** wonderful
**Adverbs of frequency:** always, never, sometimes, early
**Expressions:** I never miss it!

## Test yourself on unit 3

1. Do these exercises to check your progress.
2. Count your **correct** answers. Write the total number in the box.

**Total:** ☐ /43 correct answers

3. Try to understand your mistakes. If necessary,
   - read the **Essential Grammar**, and/or
   - look at the Student Book lesson again, or
   - ask your teacher.
4. How do you feel about this unit? Tick (✓) a box.

☐ ☐ ☐ ☐ ☐

*I can ... talk about a person's habits and routine.* Lesson 3F

**1** Rewrite the sentences with the adverbs in brackets.

1 Jennifer Lopez sings in English, but she sings in Spanish, too. (usually / sometimes)

______________________________

______________________________

2 Li Yung's an excellent student. She goes to class. She's late. (always / never)

______________________________

______________________________

3 I don't like alcohol. I drink wine or beer, but I drink champagne. (never /sometimes)

______________________________

______________________________

4 Emily wears jeans to work. She wears a suit. (never / always)

______________________________

______________________________

*I can ... make requests and suggestions.* Lesson 3A

**2** Complete the sentences with *can I*, *can you* or *let's*. Be careful with question marks (?).

1 ________ ________ sit here for a minute, please? I'm tired.

2 I love your lasagne! ________ ________ tell me how to make it?

3 It's cold tonight. ________ stay at home and watch TV.

4 A: ________ ________ play tennis?
B: Yes, I can, very well.
A: Good. OK ________ play a game on Sunday.

5 I don't have a pencil. ________ ________ lend me a pen, please?

6 I'm really busy. ________ ________ answer the phone, please?

*I can ... talk about somebody I know.* Lesson 3B

**3** Read the text. Circle the correct option.

Batman is a famous American superhero. (1)*His / Her* real name is Bruce Wayne and he (2)*live / lives* in Gotham City. He (3)*don't / can't* fly but he's very strong and he (4) *use / uses* technology to (5)*stop / stops* bad people. He (6)*wear / wears* a black suit. He (7)*don't / doesn't* wear glasses and his best (8)*friend / friend's* name is Robin.

**4** Correct the sentences.

1 Elton John plays the guitar.
*He doesn't play the guitar. He plays the piano.*

2 Queen Elizabeth II speaks Chinese.

______________________________

3 The American president lives in New York.

______________________________

4 Spider-Man works as a dentist.

______________________________

5 The American company IBM makes soft drinks.

______________________________

*I can ... have a dialogue about somebody.* Lesson 3C

**5** 3.10 Complete the dialogue. Each ✻ = one word. Listen and check.

**Kelly:** Rob, this new website has the perfect match for you.

**Rob:** Really?!? Tell me about her.

**Kelly:** OK, listen. Her name is Olga and she's 24.

**Rob:** Hmm ... What ✻ ✻ do? (1) *What does she do?*

**Kelly:** She's a professional tennis player!

**Rob:** Wow! Where ✻ ✻ live? (2) ____________

**Kelly:** ✻ ✻ ✻ Monaco. (3) ____________

**Rob:** ✻ ✻ single? (4) ____________

**Kelly:** Yes, she is.

**Rob:** Great. ✻ ✻ like to travel? (5) ____________

**Kelly:** Yes, ✻ ✻ (6) ____________

**Rob:** ✻ ✻ cook? (7) ____________

**Kelly:** Yes, she does. She ✻ Japanese food. (8) ____________

**Rob:** Mmm! ✻ ✻ read a lot? (9) ____________

**Kelly:** No, but she ✻ ✻ music. (10) ____________

**Rob:** Great!!

*I can ... ask and tell the time.* Lesson 3D

**6** Complete the dialogue.

**Rick:** Let's (1) *watch* TV. Do you like comedies?

**Rose:** Yes, I love them.

**Rick:** Me, (2) ________ ! Let's (3) ________ at the TV guide.

**Rose:** OK, let me see ... . Oh! *The Office*!

**Rick:** (4) ________ 's it (5) ________ ?

**Rose:** It's (6) ________ tonight after the news.

**Rick:** (7) ________ time (8) ________ it start?

**Rose:** Let me check. It (9) ________ (10) ________ quarter past eight.

**Rick:** Oh, no. My sister's birthday party starts at eight o'clock. What (11) ________ does it (12) ________ ?

**Rose:** It finishes (13) ________ ten to nine.

**Rick:** Great, that's perfect! It's OK if I'm an hour late.

*I can ... ask and answer about different people.* Lesson 3E

**7** Complete the questions with *does*, *where*, *what* or *what time*.
Write the answers with the words in brackets.

1 A: *What language does* your girlfriend study? (German)
B: *She studies German.*

2 A: ________ ________ Peter have breakfast? (at home}
B: He ____________ .

3 A: ________ ________ Matthew do at weekends? (play golf)
B: He ____________ .

4 A: ________ ________ Amanda go to bed? (10.45)
B: ____________ .

**8** Complete questions for the answers.

1 *What time does* Bob *get up* ?
He gets up at ten o'clock.

2 ________ ________ Bob work?
He ________ at home.

3 ________ ________ his wife ________ ?
She works for a mobile phone company.

4 ________ ________ Bob ________ after work?
He does exercise.

5 ________ ________ his wife ________ for breakfast?
She has bacon and eggs.

*I can ... say 100 more words in English* Lessons 3A–3F

**9** Cover the words and test yourself on ...

1 WB Adjectives (p. 72) Can you remember the 9 adjectives?

2 WB The time (p. 73) Can you say all the times and remember the time expressions, too?

3 WB Everyday activities (p. 74) Can you describe the man's typical day?

4 WB The alphabet (p. 69) Can you pronounce the 7 sounds and example words?

5 Phrasebook 3 (p. 78) Look at your translations. Can you translate and say the phrases in English?

# Have a good trip!

## Vocabulary

**Word Bank 12:** Around town p. 75

**Nouns:** the capital (city), a festival, a platform, population, a return, a single, a ticket, a tourist attraction, a Tourist Information Centre

**Adjectives:** exciting, main (attractions), modern

**Verbs:** open, close, finish, leave, arrive

**Expressions:** Have a good trip! How much (is it)? Just a second. You're welcome. What time does the next train leave? It takes about five hours.

p.47 **1** Circle the correct option.

**A:** What time (1)___ the next train to Cardiff (2)___, please?

**B:** It (3)___ at 6 p.m. from platform three.

**A:** What time (4)___ the banks usually open and close?

**B:** They (5)___ at 9.30 a.m. from Monday to Friday and (6)___ at 3.30 p.m.

1 a do b (does) c leaves
2 a does b leaves c leave
3 a does b leave c leaves
4 a opens b do c does
5 a opens b open c close
6 a opens b open c close

**2** Change the sentences with the words in brackets.

1 The main shopping centres close at 9 p.m. (not)
*The main shopping centres don't close at 9 p.m.*

2 What time do the museums open on Monday? (the post office)
______________________________

3 Munich has great art galleries. (Munich / not / beach)
______________________________

4 The Tourist Information Centre closes at 10.00 p.m. (does / open / weekends?)
______________________________

5 What time do the night buses leave? (the Eurostar)
______________________________

**3** 4.1 Complete the questions with the phrases. Listen and check.

the train leave · the station close · do they have · does the next · you get home · usually get the train · does the train · Underground stations close

1 What time does *the station close* tonight?
2 What time do ______________ at night?
3 ______________ bus leave Oxford at 10.27?
4 What time do you ______________ in the morning?
5 What time do ______________ after work?
6 What platform does ______________ from?
7 ______________ drinks and snacks on the train?
8 ______________ have a wifi service?

**4** 4.2 Listen and write the answers to questions 1–8 in Exercise 3.

1 *One o'clock in the morning.*
2 ______________
3 ______________
4 ______________
5 ______________
6 ______________
7 ______________
8 ______________

**5** 4.3 Complete the dialogue. Listen and check.

**Man:** Can I help you, sir?
**Tom:** Yes, please. I (1)__________ a ticket to Brighton.
**Man:** Would you like a (2)__________ or a (3)__________?
**Tom:** Single, please. How much (4)__________ __________?
**Man:** £27.80.
**Tom:** Here you are.
**Man:** Thank you. (5)__________ your ticket.
**Tom:** What time (6)__________ the next train leave?
**Man:** It (7)__________ at 11.30 from (8)__________ 5.
**Tom:** And what time does it (9)__________ in Brighton?
**Man:** At 12.45. (10)__________ a good trip!

# When's your birthday?



## Vocabulary

**Months:** January, February, March, April, May, June, July, August, September, October, November, December

**Types of music:** classical, country, heavy metal, jazz, opera, pop, rock

**Nouns:** a concert, the year 2008 (two thousand and eight)

**Ordinal numbers:** first, second, third, fourth, fifth, sixth, seventh, eighth, ninth, tenth, eleventh, twelfth, thirteenth, twentieth, twenty-first, twenty-second, twenty-third, thirtieth

**Expressions:** (on) Christmas Day / Independence Day / New Year's Eve    When's your birthday?

**1** Write the dates in two ways.

1 04/01 – *the fourth of January* ______ *4th January* ______
2 31/03 – ____________________ ____________
3 28/12 – ____________________ ____________
4 20/08 – ____________________ ____________

.49 **2** Complete the text with *in*, *on* or *when*.

Labour Day (1)_______ the USA is (2)_______ the first Monday (3)_______ September, but (4)_______ other countries it's (5)_______ 1st May.

International Mother's Day is (6)_______ 11th May. (7)_______ Mexico and much of Latin America Mother's Day is (8)_______ 10th May. (9)_______ France and Sweden Mother's Day is (10)_______ the last Sunday (11)_______ May. (12)_______ Argentina Mother's Day comes (13)_______ the second Sunday (14)_______ October.

**3** Look at the map of the New York City bus tour and complete the information.

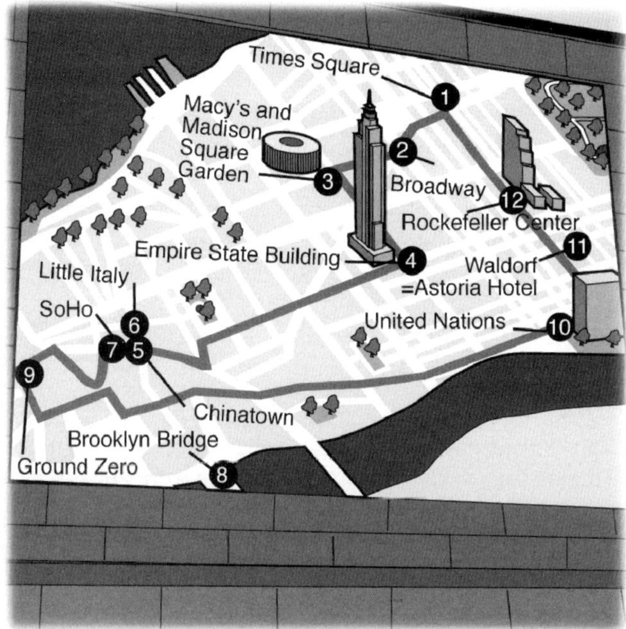


a Times Square is the *first* stop.
b SoHo is the ______________ stop.
c Brooklyn Bridge is the ______________ stop.
d Rockefeller Center is the ______________ stop.
e ______________ is the second stop.
f The ______________ stop is Ground Zero.
g The Waldorf is the ______________ stop.
h ______________ is the sixth stop.
i The ______________ stop is the United Nations.

**4** (4.4) Listen and check. Copy the pronunciation of the place names. How long do they have at each stop?

**5** Complete the crossword with months and ordinal numbers. Use the numbers in brackets.

**ACROSS**
1 ... Century Fox is a famous American film company.
3 In the USA and Europe children start school in ... .
6 October is the ... month of the year.
7 George W. Bush was the ... president of the USA. (43rd)
8 Gordon Brown is the ... British Prime Minister. (75th)
9 In South America children start school in ... .
10 Tennessee is the ... state of the USA. (16th)

**DOWN**
1 December is the ... month.
2 North Dakota is the ... state of the USA. (39th)
4 The last day of the year is ... December.
5 *I* is the first person, *you* the second and *he*, *she*, *it* are the ... person in English grammar.
6 Slovenia is the ... European country to start to use the euro. (13th)

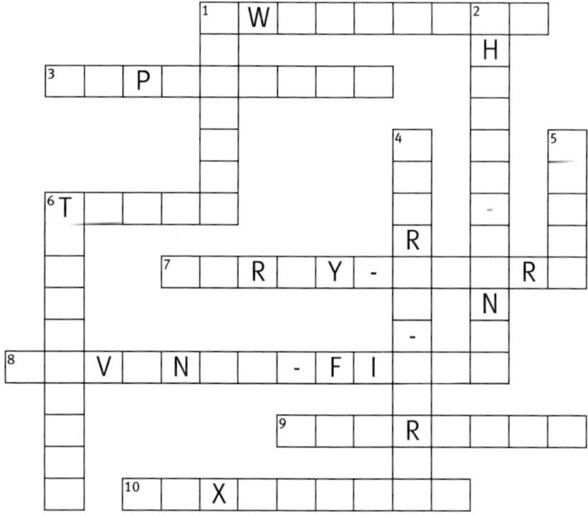

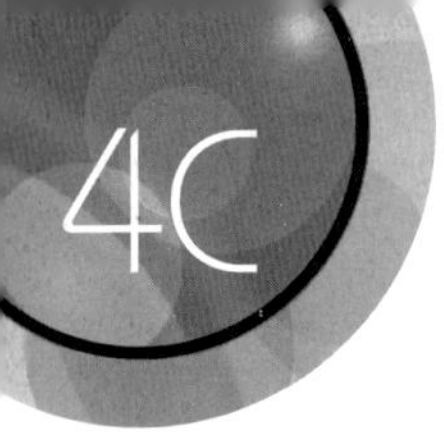


# Musicals? I'm sorry, I really hate them

## Vocabulary

**Types of films:** action films, cartoons, comedies, drama films, musicals, science fiction films, thrillers, westerns

**Object pronouns:** me, you, him, her, it, us, them

**Adjectives of opinion:** boring, fabulous

**Verbs:** love, hate

**Other:** more

**Expressions:** Come on! What do you think of ...?

**1** Find 12 words: music, film and adjectives of opinion.

| | | | | | | | | | | |
|---|---|---|---|---|---|---|---|---|---|---|
| F | P | T | W | E | S | T | E | R | N | W |
| A | C | S | T | E | C | H | N | O | M | O |
| B | Z | O | C | D | D | R | C | U | R | N |
| U | I | H | O | R | R | I | B | L | E | D |
| L | V | R | M | A | J | L | E | H | G | E |
| O | N | D | E | M | A | L | E | A | G | R |
| U | U | I | D | A | Z | E | D | T | A | F |
| S | S | S | Y | U | Z | R | R | Y | E | U |
| E | X | C | E | L | L | E | N | T | P | L |
| W | Y | O | B | S | I | N | T | U | A | H |

p.51 **2** Complete the sentences with an object pronoun.

1 Westerns? I hate _______.

2 Brad Pitt's my favourite actor. Do you like _______?

3 Opera? I love _______.

4 Mariah Carey is great. I love _______.

5 My husband and I have three dogs. They love _______.

6 I have two tickets for the concert. Do you want to come with _______?

7 Good morning, sir. Welcome to Harrods. How can I help _______ today?

**3** Circle the correct option.

1 Mario has a new job at the shopping centre. Let's visit *he / him* this afternoon.

2 Where's your wife? *She / Her* 's really late.

3 Can you call Larry after work? *He / Him* has something important to tell you.

4 On Sundays I usually play football with my friends. Why don't you come and play with *we / us*?

5 **A:** Do you know where my glasses are? I can't see *it / them*.

**B:** Are *they / them* on the table? You usually put *they / them* there.

**4** (4.5) Complete the sentences with the words. Listen and check.

hates comedies love boring fabulous

1 I love New York! It's exciting, fast and busy. It's _______________.

2 We hate _______________ . We prefer dramas.

3 I think Celine Dion's _______________. I like Amy Winehouse more.

4 My sister _______________ jazz.

5 My favourite TV channel is Discovery. I _______________ documentaries, you see.

**5** Use the words to make sentences.

1 Heavy metal / horrible / hate

*I think heavy metal is horrible. I hate it.*

2 Musicals / boring / not like

_______________

3 Woody Allen's comedies / fabulous / love

_______________

4 Old American Westerns / interesting / like

_______________

5 George Clooney / (your opinion)

_______________

6 The Rolling Stones / (your opinion)

_______________

**Study tip**

**Music in English**

You can learn a lot of English by listening to songs and singing the words. Listen and read the words of songs on CDs or read the subtitles on DVDs. Or you can find the words on the Internet, for example, using Google or at www.lyrics.com. And you can usually watch them on YouTube.com, too.

Try to listen to English music when you're in your car, when you're online or when you're cooking. The more you listen, the more you learn.

# Swimming is my favourite activity!

## Vocabulary

**Word Bank 13:** Free-time activities p. 76 **Adjectives:** recreational, silent
**Nouns:** an activity, athletics, calories, an event, a kilometre, an Olympic medal
**Verbs:** prefer (X) to (Y), lose weight
**Expressions:** I love it! I hate it! No, not really.

**1** Make sentences with the *–ing* form.

1 ___Boxing___ (box) is a dangerous sport.
2 ______________ (cycle) is good exercise.
3 ______________ (chat) online is fine, but I prefer ______________ (talk) on the phone.
4 Charles likes ______________ (run) in the park in the morning.
5 ______________ (smoke) is bad for you.
6 ______________ (drive) a taxi all day is very tiring.
7 My mother's ______________ (cook) is fantastic.

**2** Complete the sentences with the words in brackets.

1 My partner and I love ___cooking___ for our friends. We ___cook___ very well! (cook / cooking)
2 I _________ a lot because I think _________ is a wonderful activity. (read / reading)
3 My sister _________ a lot, but she hates _________ in the evenings and at weekends. (works / working)
4 _________ is great exercise. That's why I _________ every day. (walk / walking)
5 My friends and I love _________ to music. We _________ to the radio all the time. (listen / listening)
6 When I retire I want to _________ around the world. _________ is wonderful when you have time to do it slowly. (travel / travelling)

**3** (4.6) Read the text and circle the correct option. Listen and check.

Samuel and Jane want to live to be 100 years old and always think about their health. They don't (1)*drive / driving* to work, they prefer (2)*walk / walking* or (3)*cycle / cycling*. After work, they don't usually (4)*go / going* home – they stop at the gym and (5)*swim / swimming* a kilometre. (6)*Watch / Watching* TV is never in their plans, but sometimes they (7)*see / seeing* a movie, but only if they (8)*walk / walking* to the cinema and home again. (9)*Meet / Meeting* their friends on Fridays and (10)*go / going* out on Saturday nights are their favourite ways to relax and have fun.

**4** Write sentences about Jimmy using verbs 1–4.

eat ☺
walk in the ☹
watch
eat ☹☹

1 like: ___Jimmy___________________________
2 (not) like: ______________________________
3 love: ______________________________
4 hate: ______________________________

**5** Read Jimmy's answers and tick (✓) the correct questions, a or b.

1 a ☐ Let's have dinner at Fruit & Salads tonight!
  b ☐ Let's have dinner at McDonald's tonight!
**Jimmy:** That's a great idea!

2 a ☐ Do you do exercise?
  b ☐ Do you watch TV a lot?
**Jimmy:** Yes, I love it!

3 a ☐ Do you like walking?
  b ☐ Do you like sleeping after lunch?
**Jimmy:** No, not really.

4 a ☐ Do you play video games?
  b ☐ Do you eat lots of fruit?
**Jimmy:** Oh, I think it's horrible!

**6** (4.7) Listen and check.

# He goes running once a week

## Vocabulary

**Nouns:** an advert, a diet, a lifestyle, (a healthy) mind / body
**Verbs and activities:** do sit-ups, do weight training, do yoga, go on a diet
**Expressions of frequency:** once / twice / three times (a year), every (month), every other (day), regularly
**Question word:** How often ...?

**1** Match two activities to each verb.

computer games skiing weight training on a diet ballet basketball

1 Go ______
2 Play ______
3 Do ______

p.55 **2** Write *How often ...?* questions and answers about Anna's six activities.

| Anna's week | S | M | T | W | T | F | S |
|---|---|---|---|---|---|---|---|
| tennis | | ✓ | | ✓ | | | |
| yoga | ✓ | ✓ | ✓ | ✓ | ✓ | ✓ | ✓ |
| running | | | ✓ | | | | |
| weight training | | ✓ | | ✓ | | ✓ | |
| volleyball | | | | | | ✓ | |
| aerobics | ✓ | | ✓ | | ✓ | ✓ | |

1 *How often does Anna play tennis?*
*She plays tennis twice a week.*
2 ______
3 ______
4 ______
5 ______
6 ______

**3** Look at Diana's breakfast plan. Complete the text.

*Breakfast*
*Mon cereal*
*Tue fruit & coffee*
*Wed cereal*
*Thur fruit*
*Fri cereal & coffee*
*Sat fruit*
*Sun bacon and eggs & coffee*

What (1)______ Diana usually (2)______ for (3)______? (4)______ breakfast, she has cereal or fruit (5)______ ______ day. She has bacon and eggs (6)______ a week on (7)______. She only has coffee (8)______ ______ ______ ______. She (9)______ eats sausages or fries.

**4** Add the missing word to each sentence.

1 I *go* running three times a week.
2 My friends and I dancing once week.
3 My wife and I a special dinner twice a month.
4 I don't often go concerts.
5 Doing aerobics excellent exercise.

**5** (4.8) Get out of the maze. Number the blocks from 1–25. Move ↑, →, ↓, and ←.

| | | | | |
|---|---|---|---|---|
| *1* Ray Hills | *2* is | he | always | goes out with |
| has | *3* 24 years old. | *10* the weekend | At | *14* his |
| sometimes | *4* He | loves sport | every morning. | girlfriend. |
| a little | Never | and he | plays tennis | *16* They |
| running | usually | swim | go dancing | don't usually |
| going | like | *20* they | but | goes dancing |
| to the cinema | or to the theatre | work | when | in the evening |
| very well | *25* a lot. | prefers | twice a week | shopping |

Write a paragraph about Ray from blocks 1–25. Listen and check.

*Ray Hills is 24 years old. He ...*

# We hardly ever go to bed early

## Vocabulary

**Nouns:** a couple, a rule
**Adjective:** funny
**Expressions:** I love them! I don't really like her. I really like him. I know him! Who's she? Only joking!
**Expressions of frequency:** hardly ever, often
**Question word:** Which?

## Test yourself on unit 4

1. Do these exercises to check your progress.
2. Count your **correct** answers. Write the total number in the box.

   **Total:** ☐ /37 correct answers

3. Try to understand your mistakes. If necessary,
   - read the **Essential Grammar**, and/or
   - look at the Student Book lesson again, or
   - ask your teacher.
4. How do you feel about this unit? Tick (✓) a box.

   ☐ ☐ ☐ ☐ ☐

*I can ... talk about a person's habits and routine.* Lesson 4F

**1** Make long sentences with the two adverbs in brackets.

1 Sandy plays tennis, but she plays in the morning. (every day of the week / hardly ever)
*Sandy plays tennis every day of the week, but she hardly ever plays in the morning.*

2 Vince spends his evenings at home, but he goes out. (every month / sometimes)
______

3 I arrive at work late because my boss is on time. (often / hardly ever)
______

4 Evelyn drinks a lot of tea, but she take sugar or milk. (every day / not usually)
______

5 I do exercise and I'm on a diet. (every other day / often)
______

*I can ... talk about opening hours.* Lesson 4A

**2** Write true sentences about where you live with the words in brackets.

1 Supermarkets usually ______ from Monday to Saturday. (open at)

2 The post office near my house ______ at ______. (close)

3 Most restaurants ______ (finish) serving food at ______.

4 My favourite shop ______ (open) on Sundays.

*I can ... use prepositions correctly.* Lesson 4B

**3** Complete the sentences with *at*, *in*, *on* or *to*.

1 See you (1)_____ the morning.

2 **A:** Let's meet (2)_____ the weekend. Are you free (3)_____ Saturday afternoon (4)_____ about 3 o'clock?
**B:** Sorry. I can't. That's when I work. Can we meet (5)_____ Saturday night (6)_____ about 10.30?
**A:** No, I can't do that. I have to stay (7)_____.
**A:** OK, so what do you want to do tonight?
**B:** Let's go (8)_____ the cinema.

*I can ... use object pronouns* Lesson 4C

**4** Rewrite the sentences using a pronoun or for the underlined word(s). Use contractions.

1 I love Abba.
*I love them.*

2 James thinks you are special.
*He thinks you're special.*

3 I am in love with Leo.
______

4 Romantic comedies are boring.
______

5 This book is fantastic!

___

6 I think about Vanessa every day.

___

7 You send text messages to your friends every hour!

___

8 Mum always tells me and my sister to eat slowly.

___

*I can ... talk about activities* Lesson 4D

**5** Complete the text with the correct form of the verbs in brackets.

## Waikiki Oahu Beach Resort

Do you love activity holidays or do you prefer (1)____ (relax) on the beach? Waikiki Oahu Beach Resort has a special package for everybody of every age.

### Paradise Plus

Do you like (2)____ (spend) days on the beach and (3)____ (swim) with your family? Then in the evening, you can (4)____ (have) a romantic dinner in our 5-star restaurant without your children. Our qualified babysitters love (5)____ (play) with children and always (6)____ (give) them an evening to remember!

### Surf's Up

Is (7)____ (surf) your favourite sport? Every year, surfers from all over the world (8)____ (come) for Hawaii's international events. Don't forget your surfboard! Special classes for beginners. Enjoy (9)____ (shop) in our beautiful boutiques every day from 10 a.m. to 10 p.m. We (10)____ (have) some great souvenirs for you.

| | | | |
|---|---|---|---|
| 1 | *relaxing* | 6 | ___ |
| 2 | ___ | 7 | ___ |
| 3 | ___ | 8 | ___ |
| 4 | ___ | 9 | ___ |
| 5 | ___ | 10 | ___ |

*I can ... ask and answer about frequency.* Lesson 4E

**6** Look at the information and write sentences about Jonas's routine.

**Sunday**
✔ Ball games in the park
✔ Lunch with mum
✔ Watch the news

**Monday**
✔ Spanish lessons
✔ Cook dinner

**Tuesday**
✔ Karate
✔ Cook dinner

**Wednesday**
✔ Spanish lessons
✔ Cook dinner

**Thursday**
✔ Karate
✔ Cook dinner

**Friday**
✔ Spanish lessons
✔ Dinner in a restaurant

**Saturday**
✔ Ball games in the park
✔ Go out dancing

1 have dinner at a restaurant
*Jonas has dinner at a restaurant once a week.*

2 play a ball game in the park

___

3 cook dinner

___

4 lunch with mum

___

5 do karate

___

6 have Spanish lessons

___

7 go out dancing

___

*I can ... say 150 more words in English* Lessons 4A–4F

**7** Cover the words and test yourself on ...

1 WB Around town (p. 75) Can you remember the 27 places?

2 (p. 48) Can you pronounce the 12 months and the 31 days correctly?

3 (p. 50) Remember and pronounce correctly 8 types of films and 8 types of music.

4 WB Free time activities (p. 76) Remember and spell the 12 different activities.

5 WB (p. 69) Can you pronounce the vowel sounds and example words?

6 Phrasebook 4 (p. 78) Look at your translations. Can you say the phrases in English?

## Student's book

### 1.18 1D Exercise 1

**Tim:** Hey, Anna. Good evening.
**Anna:** Tim! Hi! How are you?
**Tim:** I'm fine. Sorry I'm late!
**Anna:** Oh, that's OK. Let me introduce you. Kate, this is my friend Tim Grant.
**Kate:** Hello, Tim. Nice to meet you.
**Tim:** Nice to meet you too, Kate.

### 1.23 1E Exercise 1

**Kate:** So, Tim. Are you and Anna just friends?
**Tim:** Me and Anna? Yes, we're friends. We're journalists – we're on a project together.
**Kate:** Oh, I see. And, are you married?
**Tim:** No, I'm divorced. What about you? Are you married?
**Kate:** Married? No way! I'm single.
**Tim:** And ... what do you do?
**Kate:** I'm an actress.
**Tim:** Really? Are you famous?
**Kate:** No, I'm not! But I'm in one or two television commercials.
**Tim:** Wow! That's interesting!

### 1.29 1F Exercise 2

Oh hi Rita ... it's Lars ... please come to my birthday party at eight o'clock on Friday ... that's eight o'clock on Friday. The party is at the Elephant's Head E-L-E-P-H-A-N-T apostrophe S H-E-A-D and the address is 224 Camden High Street and that's in Camden. OK – 224 Camden High Street, the Elephant's Head. ... and my home number is 020 908 745 – 020 908 745 OK? My work phone number's 01453 399522. That's 01453 399522. And my mobile phone number is 79663 289851. That's 79663 289851. So please call me and ... See you on Friday. Bye.

### 1.31 1F Exercise 6

**Anna:** Hmmm ... This is very good food!
**Leo:** Well, yes, it's not bad.
**Tim:** So where are you from, Leo?
**Leo:** I'm British, from York, in England.
**Kate:** And what do you do?
**Leo:** I'm a chef.
**Anna:** A chef? Really? Like in a restaurant?
**Leo:** Yes, that's right. *My* restaurant! Italian food!
**Anna:** Italian. Like me. Wow!
**Leo:** Look. This is my card. Come and visit the restaurant!
**Anna:** Thanks. Little Italy. That's nice. 409 Harley Street, Camden. Good!
**Leo:** And here's my mobile number: 07723 867982. Here's a pen. 07723 867982. Please call me.
**Anna:** Oh! Thank you!
**Leo:** But I don't have your number, Anna! Do you have a mobile?

### 1.35 Revision 1 Exercise 10

Hi everybody! We're Laura Bernard and Raphael Petit. We're French and we live in Lyon. We're lawyers and we work for the same company.

We love Lyon. We think it's an excellent city. Come and contact us! Our work number is 3771-4563 and our home address is 1483 ...

### 2.3 2A Exercise 6

**Agent:** Good morning, Mr and Mrs Wang. It's W-A-N-G, right?
**Mrs W:** Yes, that's right. W-A-N-G. Wang.
**Agent:** Thank you. OK. Here's your programme.
**Mr W:** Thank you.
**Agent:** On Sunday evening you're on flight AA3315 from New York JFK to Rome.
**Mrs W:** AA3315 to Rome. OK. So we're in Italy on Monday. Great!
**Mr W:** Thank you.
**Agent:** On Tuesday and Wednesday you're in Madrid. Olé!
**Mrs W:** Good! We're in Spain.
**Mr W:** Thank you.
**Agent:** On Thursday and Friday, it's Paris.
**Mr W:** We're in France on Thursday and Friday. Fantastic!
**Agent:** Then on Saturday morning you go to England by Eurostar. It's an excellent train service.
**Mrs W:** OK. We're in England on Saturday.
**Mr W:** Thank you.
**Agent:** And your flight from London to New York is number DL0293. That's from Heathrow Airport in London. Flight number 0293. Happy?
**Mr W:** Thank you very much.
**Agent:** No probem. Have a good holiday.

### 2.6 2B Exercise 3

**Leo:** ... chat show's very good, and I think she's excellent!
**Anna:** Yes, she is. I agree. How old is she?
**Leo:** I think she's about 55.
**Anna:** 55 years old? Wow! She looks great! Is she an actress?
**Leo:** No, she isn't. Not now, anyway, but remember... ... people love him. They say he's very attractive.
**Anna:** He is! He's fantastic! Where's he from? He isn't English, is he?
**Leo:** No, he's from Scotland.
**Anna:** Is he a singer, too?
**Leo:** No. Well, he sings in *Moulin Rouge*, but I don't ...

### (2.9) 2C Exercise 6

1 What's his address? What's his mobile number?
2 What's their e-mail address? What's their phone number?
3 What's her address? What's her home number?

### (2.11) 2D Exercise 2

**Tim:** Jane, my ex-wife, lives in Australia. She's a lawyer.
**Kate:** Oh, I see. Do you have children?
**Tim:** Yes, I do. I have a son and two daughters ... I have a photo here ... Just a moment. Ah, yes, here it is!
**Kate:** Oh, what a nice photo!
**Tim:** Yes. These are Melanie and Jessica, my daughters.
**Kate:** They're lovely. How old are they?
**Tim:** Melanie's 9 and Jessica's 7. Melanie's very big now. She's about one metre fifty.
**Kate:** Wow!
**Tim:** Yes, but Jessica is small, like her mother.
**Kate:** And what's your son's name?
**Tim:** Stephen. Or Steve for short.
**Kate:** Steve. That's a nice name. How old is he?
**Tim:** 11.
**Kate:** And who are the other people?
**Tim:** Well, this is my little brother Mark, and this is my sister-in-law. Her name's Inés. They're both actors.
**Kate:** You have a nice family, Tim.
**Tim:** Thanks.
**Kate:** Do you live alone in London?
**Tim:** No, I don't. I live with my son.
**Kate:** How nice!
**Tim:** Yes. He's here in London with me now. Steve's a great boy. What about you, Kate? Do you have a big family?
**Kate:** No, I don't. I only have my father and one sister.
**Tim:** Oh, I see ...

### (2.14) 2E Exercise 3

**A** I like children a lot.
**B** I don't play football.
**C** I have a nice car.
**D** I work for a successful company.
**E** I don't smoke.
**F** I speak Spanish very well.

### (2.16) 2E Exercise 5 Part 1

**Jane:** Hi W-guy!
**W-guy:** Hello JaneG.
**Jane:** You can call me Jane. Can you tell me your real name?
**W-guy:** Sorry?
**Jane:** What's your real name? W ... Walter? Wesley?
**W-guy:** William. William Walker. But you can call me Will.
**Jane:** Thanks. How old are you, Will?
**W-guy:** I'm 34.
**Jane:** Can I ask you some questions?
**W-guy:** Of course!

### (2.19) 2F Exercise 3

**Jane:** I love your car, Larry! It's beautiful!
**Larry:** Well, thanks. I like my two Mercedes a lot!
**Jane:** Two Mercedes? You have *two* Mercedes?
**Larry:** Yes, the car ... and the cat.
**Jane:** Oh! Do you have a cat?
**Larry:** Yes, I do. Her name's Mercedes. What about you? Any pets?
**Jane:** Well, my children have a goldfish. You see, I live in a small house. Where do you live?
**Larry:** In a flat. I live in a big flat in Bondi.
**Jane:** Bondi! Wow! That's a very nice place!
**Larry:** Yes, it is. I like it a lot!
**Jane:** And where do you work?
**Larry:** I work for Wilson & Johnson. It's an American law office.
**Jane:** Where's that?
**Larry:** Oh, it's in the city centre. In Pitt Street. About 200 metres from the Opera House. Do you know it?
**Jane:** No, no. I'm new here, remember?
**Larry:** Me too ... I'm from New York! OK. Come on. Let's go and see Sydney!
**Jane:** Larry!

### (2.21) 2F Exercise 6

**Jane:** Please stop! Thank you, Larry.
**Larry:** No problem, Jane.
**Jane:** So, Larry, I know you don't like sports ...
**Larry:** Oh, no, no. I don't like *football*, but I like sports!
**Jane:** Really?
**Larry:** Yes, I play tennis on Friday evening.
**Jane:** I see ...
**Larry:** And I play volleyball on Saturday morning.
**Jane:** Great! And what else do you do at the weekend?
**Larry:** On Saturday I usually go to the cinema in the evening.
**Jane:** And what do you do on Sunday?
**Larry:** Well, in the morning I usually spend some time online – watching YouTube movies. I love that! And in the afternoon I study Spanish!
**Jane:** Oh really? Say something in Spanish to me!
**Larry:** OK, erm ... Me gusta mucho el YouTube.

### (3.12) 3D Exercise 1

**Tim:** Phew! I'm really tired! Let's stop now, Anna!
**Anna:** OK. That's fine. What time is it, Tim?
**Tim:** It's twenty past seven.
**Anna:** Oh no! I'm late! Really late! Look at the time! I have to go home now!
**Tim:** Why?

**Anna:** It's ... my favourite TV programme ... It starts at seven-thirty.
**Tim:** Hmm. What is it?
**Anna:** Well, erm ... It's erm ... *EastEnders* ...
**Tim:** A soap opera? No! Do you like soap operas?
**Anna:** Yes, they're great! Well, I am from Italy! Italians love soap operas! Bye!
**Tim:** See you tomorrow!

### 3.15 3D Exercise 8

**Vicki:** What about you, Tim? Do *you* have a favourite TV programme?
**Tim:** Me? A TV programme? No, I don't have a favourite ... .
**Vicki:** Really? No favourite at all?
**Tim:** Well, I kind of like *ER*, I guess.
**Vicki:** *ER*? When is it on?
**Tim:** On Thursdays – on Channel Four.
**Vicki:** Sorry. What channel's it on?
**Tim:** On Channel Four.
**Vicki:** I see. What time does it start?
**Tim:** At 10 p.m. It ends at 11.
**Vicki:** Wait a minute! I know *ER*! It's like a medical soap opera, isn't it?
**Tim:** No, it's not a soap opera! No way! It's ... different!
**Vicki:** It's a soap opera. Of course it is!
**Tim:** No, it isn't!

### 3.18 3F Exercise 1

**Anna:** Hello.
**Kate:** Hi, Anna. Kate here.
**Anna:** Oh, hi Kate!
**Kate:** Listen, let's have dinner together – you and me and Tim and Leo.
**Anna:** That's a good idea. Where?
**Kate:** How about Gordon Ramsay's?
**Anna:** Wow! That's great! Leo loves good food!
**Kate:** Good. Can you phone and make a reservation, please? I'm really, really busy!
**Anna:** Oh, sure! No problem! What time?
**Kate:** Is eight fifteen OK?
**Anna:** Great! See you later.

### 4.3 4A Exercise 3

**Lars:** Hello.
**W:** Thank you for calling the Edinburgh Tourist Information Centre.
**Lars:** Hello.
**W:** I'm sorry, but we're closed.
**Lars:** Oh!
**W:** The Centre opens Monday to Wednesday from 9 a.m. to 5 p.m. and from 9 a.m. to 6 p.m. on Thursday, Friday and Saturday. On Sundays, we open at 10 a.m. and close at 5 p.m.
**Lars:** OK.
**W:** Thank you for calling the Edinburgh Tourist Information Centre. Goodbye.
**Lars:** Goodbye.

### 4.4 4A Exercise 4

**W:** Good morning. Welcome to the London Tourist Information Centre. Can I help you?
**Lars:** Hello. Yes, please. Do you have information about Edinburgh?
**W:** Edinburgh? Yes, I think we do. Just a second. Where are you from?
**Lars:** Sweden.
**W:** Ah, Sweden, that's nice. OK, here are some brochures for you. Is that OK?
**Lars:** Thank you. I have some questions for you about Edinburgh.
**W:** OK. What would you like to know?
**Lars:** Well, what time do the big shops open on Sundays?
**W:** The big shops? You mean the main shopping centres?
**Lars:** Yes, yes, what time do the shopping centres open on Sundays?
**W:** Let's have a look! Yes here. Look here in this brochure. It says all the main shopping centres open at 11 a.m. to 5 p.m. on Sundays.
**Lars:** OK ... from 11 to 5, uh-huh. And, during the week, what time do they open?
**W:** They open ... from Monday to Wednesday and on Saturday, they open at 10 a.m. and close at 6 p.m. It's late-night shopping on Thursdays and Fridays, so they close at 7.30 p.m.
**Lars:** Sorry, my English is not very good. Can you say that again, please, more slowly?
**W:** OK, no problem. Look here. It says on Monday, Tuesday and Wednesday and on Saturday, they open at 10 a.m. and close at 6 p.m. And on Thursdays and Fridays it's late-night shopping. So, they close at 7.30 p.m. OK?
**Lars:** Great! Thanks. And what about the ... post office?
**W:** It opens at 9 a.m. and closes at 5.30 p.m. – every day except on Saturday.
**Lars:** From 9 to 5.30. Good. I see. And what time does the post office close on Saturdays?
**W:** At 1 p.m.
**Lars:** Phew! Thank you. Yes!
**W:** Right. Is there anything else you would like to know?
**Lars:** No, well, yes, no ... thank you very much.
**W:** That's no problem. Bye!

### 4.10 4B Exercise 9

**Anna:** Hello.
**Emma:** Oh, hi Anna. This is Emma. How are you?
**Anna:** Fine. What's up?

**Emma:** It's Tim's birthday next week and ...
**Anna:** Really? When?
**Emma:** On Friday 4th September. Let's have a surprise party for him!
**Anna:** Sure! That's an excellent idea. How can I help?
**Emma:** Can you buy him a present?
**Anna:** Of course! Any ideas?
**Emma:** How about a CD? What type of music does he like?
**Anna:** I think he likes rock, pop and jazz.
**Emma:** I know. Let's buy him a DVD – you know, a concert on DVD.
**Anna:** Perfect!

### 4.15 4D Exercise 8

**Kate:** Anna! Hi! So you like running, too!
**Anna:** Hi, Kate! Nice to see you! Well, no! I don't really like running. Actually, I hate it! But it's good exercise, so ...
**Kate:** Oh I think it's OK, I mean I like running *some*times, but I really prefer swimming. I often go swimming in the morning.
**Anna:** Oh, yes! Swimming is fantastic. It's the best sport. In Italy I go swimming a lot, but not here in London. It's cold!
**Kate:** What about Leo? Does he like swimming, too?
**Anna:** Leo? No way! He hates it! He prefers walking and cycling. And he doesn't like running, so I usually go running alone.
**Kate:** But do you sometimes do exercise together?
**Anna:** Oh, sure! We sometimes go dancing together. Leo doesn't like dancing much, but I love it.
**Kate:** I never go dancing here ... It's terrible! I love dancing, but I don't have time, you know, I work in the evenings.
**Anna:** Yes, I know.
**Kate:** Listen, Anna. Let's go swimming together every morning. What do you think?
**Anna:** Yes, OK. That's an excellent idea.
**Kate:** Great! Come on!

### 4.16 4E Exercise 3

Hi. I'm Jim Ransom. I'm Canadian, from Toronto, but I live in California now, in Los Angeles. I'm 47 and I live alone with my two cats. I'm a computer programmer and I work for a small company here in Los Angeles.

Last year I was very unhappy: I was really fat! I was about 110 kilograms! But now, this year I'm a very happy man. I have a new body, a new look, a new life! I'm now just 65 kilograms! That's right – 45 kilos less. Fantastic! I eat a lot less than before, you know ... And I do a lot of exercise and I love it! I play tennis, I go running, I go swimming, I do yoga ... I just can't stop!

### 4.19 4F Exercise 1

**Kate:** Let's all go to the cinema.
**Anna:** Great idea, Kate! What film do you want to see?
**Kate:** How about *Casablanca*? It's on at the ABC. I really love that film.
**Tim:** Oh, no! Not *Casablanca*. I don't like black and white films very much.
**Leo:** OK, Tim. Let's go and see the new Judi Dench film.
**Anna:** Judi who? Who's she? I don't know her.
**Kate:** Anna? You don't know Judi Dench? She's a fabulous British actress!
**Leo:** Yes, she plays M in the Bond films.
**Anna:** Oh, yes, of course. She's great! Let's ...
**Tim:** Well I'm not sure. Judi Dench is a wonderful actress but, well, she's always a bit Shakespearean.
**Kate:** You mean you don't like Shakespearean actresses, Tim?
**Tim:** No, I hate them!
**Anna:** Really? Oh, well. OK, Tim. So what type of film *do* you like? Thrillers?
**Tim:** Well, thrillers, yes! I love them ... Hey, it *is* Friday night, you know. How about something with Scarlet Johannson. I like her. Or Keira Knightley? I *really* like her! Or Jessica Alba ... She's beautiful! Or Angelina Jolie, or ...!
**Kate:** Tim!! Please!
**Tim:** Only joking, Kate. Relax! Let's go and see the new Judi Dench film. I think Judi Dench is great!

### 4.23 Revision 4 Exercise 8

**Man:** So, Pia. Can I ask you one or two questions, please?
**Pia:** Sure. What would you like to know?
**Man:** Do you like swimming?
**Pia:** No, I don't. I hate it. It's really boring!
**Man:** OK. And what about cycling? Do you like that?
**Pia:** No, I'm sorry, I don't like cycling. I'm not really a sports fan.
**Man:** Oh dear. So what do you like doing, then?
**Pia:** Well, I like reading and I love dancing.
**Man:** Dancing! That's interesting.
**Pia:** Yes, I'm a very good dancer.
**Man:** Good. And what about shopping? I'm sure you like shopping.
**Pia:** No, I don't. I hate it!

## Activity book

### 2.5 2E Exercise 4

Hi. I'm 32 years old. I'm divorced and I have three children. I'm English, but I live in Sydney now. You, my perfect man, you're about 35 and you work for a big company. You have a nice car and you speak Spanish very well – I love Spanish! But, please, you don't play football, OK? And you don't smoke – it's a terrible habit.

Very important: you like children a lot!

Do you want to meet me?

### 3.2 3A Exercise 6

1 Work, work, work. 20 phone calls. 30 e-mails. Meetings all morning, interviews all afternoon, shopping, cooking and children all evening. I don't have time for coffee or friends or exercise. Aaaah! I'm ...!
2 No good programmes on TV. My friends aren't on MSN. I don't like this book. I don't like my CDs. I don't like school. I don't like anything. I don't know what to do. I'm ...!
3 I'm hot. No I'm not. Now I'm cold. Brrrrrrr! Now I'm thirsty. No, I'm not. Now I'm tired. Oooh! I'm not well. Brrrrrrr! I know. I'm ...!

### 3.4 3B Exercise 5

**Kate:** What's your husband's name, Anna?
**Anna:** Paolo. He's a writer. He's in Italy now with his family.
**Kate:** Is he a typical Italian?
**Anna:** Paolo? No, not really ... He isn't typical. For example, he doesn't like coffee. Italians love coffee, but Paolo only drinks tea.
**Kate:** What about football? Italians love football – their 'beautiful game'! Does Paolo play football?
**Anna:** No, he doesn't. And he doesn't watch football on TV. He likes volleyball.
**Kate:** Not very typical, then!
**Anna:** No! Well, a little. He loves pasta, spaghetti, white wine, you know, all Italian food!
**Kate:** Ah, OK. Me, too. I love Italian food, too.
**Anna:** Me, too. Hmm! I'm hungry. Let's go to an Italian restaurant on Saturday night!
**Kate:** OK! Good idea!

### 3.5 3C Exercise 5

1 Does she live in England? No, she doesn't. She lives in Canada.
2 Does she speak Italian? Yes, she does.
3 Does she have a job? Yes, she does.
4 Does she work at home? No, she doesn't. She works in the city centre.
5 Does she drink alcohol? No, she doesn't. She drinks water.
6 Does she have a pet? Yes, she does. She has a dog.
7 Does she like music? Yes, she does.
8 Does she do a lot at the weekend? Yes, she does.
9 Does she have a partner? Yes, she does.
10 Does she stay at home on Sunday evening? No, she doesn't. She goes to the cinema.

### 3.7 3D Exercise 4

**Doctor:** Hello, Martha. What can I do for you?
**Martha:** Doctor, I'm very busy, and very, very tired. Can you help me, please?
**Doctor:** What do you do?
**Martha:** I'm a businesswoman. I have a small business. I work alone.
**Doctor:** Well, tell me about your typical day.
**Martha:** OK. My days are very busy. I usually get up at half past five in the morning. And, at six o'clock, I watch the news on TV. Then, er, I have breakfast and I go online for about forty minutes. At a quarter to eight I drive my children to school and go to work. Then, at half past twelve, I do exercise at my sportsclub. After that, at quarter past one, I have a shower and then I have lunch. At exactly twenty past seven, I go home and have dinner with my children. Phew! Then, I do my English homework. I study a lot. And, um, I finally go to bed at one o'clock in the morning.
**Doctor:** Oh, Martha, have a holiday! Please!

### 4.4 4B Exercise 4

Welcome to the New York City bus tour. We have 12 stops on this tour. We stop for five minutes only at each stop. Times Square is the first stop. Broadway is the second stop, then Macy's and Madison Square Garden and the Empire State Building. Chinatown is the fifth stop, and Little Italy is sixth, and then SoHo. Brooklyn Bridge is the eighth stop. The ninth stop is Ground Zero. Your tenth stop is the United Nations. The Waldorf Astoria Hotel is the eleventh stop and finally, the twelfth stop is Rockefeller Center. Please remember you have only five minutes to take photos at each stop.

### 4.8 4E Exercise 5

Ray Hills is 24 years old. He loves sport and he plays tennis every morning. At the weekend, he always goes out with his girlfriend. They don't usually go dancing, but they like going to the cinema or to the theatre a lot.

# 1 Essential Grammar

**1** Complete the table with the words.

~~a~~ ~~actors~~ airport an be films good I meet nice party the you

| Adjective | Definite article | Indefinite article | Singular noun | Plural noun | Pronoun | Verb |
|---|---|---|---|---|---|---|
| 1 ______ | 3 ______ | 4 *a* | 6 ______ | 8 *actors* | 10 ______ | 12 ______ |
| 2 ______ | | 5 ______ | 7 ______ | 9 ______ | 11 ______ | 13 ______ |

## Indefinite articles: *a/an* + adjective + noun → 1A, 1E

| | | |
|---|---|---|
| **Singular** | a | This is a fantastic city.<br>I'm a student. |
| | an | This is an excellent book.<br>She's an Italian actress. |
| **Plural** | | We're good friends.<br>They're terrible students. |

## Definite article: *the* → 1B, 1D

| | | |
|---|---|---|
| **Singular** | the | Please open the door.<br>the United States |
| **Plural** | the | Look at the photos.<br>Say the new words. |

**2** Circle the correct rule.

1 Use *a* / *an* before *a, e, i, o* and *u*.
2 *Use / Don't use* ***a*** or ***an*** with plurals.
3 *Use / Don't use* ***the*** with plurals.
4 *Use / Don't use* ***the*** for a definite noun.
5 *Adjective + noun / noun + adjective* is correct in English.
6 English adjectives *have / don't have* a plural form.

## Present simple: verb *be* → 1B, 1C, 1D

| + & − | |
|---|---|
| I | 'm (not) a teacher. |
| You<br>We<br>They | are (n't) in London. |
| He<br>She<br>It | is (n't) Spanish. |

| ? | | + | | | − | | |
|---|---|---|---|---|---|---|---|
| Am | I ...? | | I | am. | | I | 'm not. |
| Are | you ...?<br>we ...?<br>they ...? | Yes, | you<br>we<br>they | are. | No, | you<br>we<br>they | aren't. |
| Is | he ...?<br>she ...?<br>it ...? | | he<br>she<br>it | is. | | he<br>she<br>it | isn't. |

| *Wh*-questions | | |
|---|---|---|
| What | 's | your name?<br>this?<br>that? |
| | are | those?<br>these? |

## *Where ... from?* → 1D

| | | |
|---|---|---|
| Where | am I<br>is he / she/ it<br>are you / we / they | from? |
| I'm<br>He / She / It's<br>You / We / They're | from | Mexico.<br>Canada.<br>France. |
| | Mexican.<br>Canadian.<br>French. | |

**3** Complete the table.

| Contraction | No contraction |
|---|---|
| I'm | I am |
| I'm not | ______ |
| ___ / She's / It's | He is not<br>______<br>______ |
| ______ | We are |
| You're not | ______ |
| They aren't | ______ |

**4** Circle the correct rule.

1 English has *6 / 7* pronouns.
2 The verb *be* has *3 / 4* (+) contractions.
3 The verb *be* has *4 / 5* (-) contractions.
4 In questions, use: *pronoun + verb be / verb be + pronoun.*
5 In negatives, use: *not + verb be / verb be + not.*
6 It's *correct / wrong* to say: *"Yes, I'm."*
7 Countries and nationalities have *small / CAPITAL* letters.
8 Jobs and classroom nouns have *small / CAPITAL* letters.
9 Names, cities and languages have *small / CAPITAL* letters.

## *This / These & That / Those* → 1C

This is my new phone, and
these are my new glasses.

No! That's my new phone, and
those are my new glasses.


**5** Complete the rule with *this*, *that*, *these* or *those*.

1 Use ________ and ________ with singular nouns.

2 Use ________ and ________ with plural nouns.

3 Use ________ and ________ for things in your hand or near you.

4 Use ________ and ________ for other things.

## Plurals → 1C, 1E

| Noun + *s* | |
|---|---|
| a book | books |
| a pen | pens |
| a student | students |
| a taxi | taxis |

| Special plurals | |
|---|---|
| box | boxes |
| actress | actresses |
| dictionary | dictionaries |
| housewife | housewives |

## *can/can't* → 1E

| | | | |
|---|---|---|---|
| + | I / He | can | drive a moped. |
| − | You / They | can't | a car. |

*Can/can't* has one positive and one negative form.

**6** Complete the table.

| Singular | Plural |
|---|---|
| an address | addresses |
| ________ | cats |
| a party | ________ |
| ________ | Americans |
| ________ | hairbrushes |
| a kiss | ________ |
| ________ | continents |
| a diary | ________ |
| a dollar | ________ |
| a capital letter | capital letters |
| a credit card | ________ |
| ________ | cities |
| a footballer | ________ |
| a number | ________ |
| ________ | Italians |

**7** Complete the table.

| Singular | Plural |
|---|---|
| This is a good hotel. | These are good hotels. |
| It's an identity card. | ________ |
| That's a magazine. | ________ |
| ________ | They're phone messages. |
| This is a mobile phone. | ________ |
| an English newspaper | ________ |
| ________ | They're nice photos. |
| He's a police officer. | ________ |
| ________ | They're Italian wallets. |
| She's a secretary. | ________ |
| It's a Japanese car. | ________ |
| ________ | We can drive. |

**1** 1 good 2 nice 3 the 5 an 6 airport 7 party 9 films 10 I 11 you 12 be 13 meet
**2** 2 Don't use 3 Use 4 Use 5 Adjective + noun 6 don't have
**3** I am not He's She is not It is not We're You are not They are not
**4** 1 7 2 3 3 4 4 verb *be* + pronoun 5 verb *be* + *not* 6 wrong 7 CAPITAL 8 small 9 CAPITAL
**5** 1 This/that 2 these/those 3 this/these 4 that/those
**6** a cat parties an American a hairbrush kisses a continent diaries dollars credit cards a city footballers high numbers Italian
**7** They're identity cards. Those are magazines. It's a phone message These are mobile phones. English newspapers It's a nice photo. They're police officers. It's an Italian wallet. They're secretaries. They're Japanese cars. I can drive.

# 2 Essential Grammar

## Prepositions → 2A, 2F

| | | | |
|---|---|---|---|
| **Days** | I play tennis | on | Tuesdays. |
| **Part of the day** | We study | in | the morning.<br>the afternoon.<br>the evening. |
| **Day + Part of the day** | I have lessons | on | Monday morning.<br>Friday afternoon. |
| ***the weekend*** | Let's meet | at | the weekend! |
| **Cities**<br>**Countries**<br>**Places**<br>**Languages** | I live<br>Are you<br>We live<br>They work<br>Say this<br>His office is | in | Milan.<br>Japan?<br>a flat.<br>the city centre.<br>English, please.<br>Shaftesbury Avenue. |
| ***home*** | Are you | at | home? |
| ***work*** | I'm | at | work. |

**1** Complete the sentence with *in*, *on* or *at*.

*See you ...*

___ Saturday. ___ work.
___ Thursday night. ___ Beijing.
___ the evening. ___ China.
___ Sunday evening. ___ home.

## Capital letters

**2** Study the preposition box. Circle the correct rule and complete the examples

1 Days of the week have *small / CAPITAL* letters.
__onday __uesday __ednesday

2 Parts of the day have *small / CAPITAL* letters.
in the __orning in the __fternoon at __ight

3 Languages have *small / CAPITAL* letters.
__hinese __apanese __ussian

4 Street names have *small / CAPITAL* letters.
__ondon __oad __xford __treet.

## *How old* + verb *be ...?* → 2B

| | | |
|---|---|---|
| How old | am I? | I'm 20. or I'm 20 years old. |
| | is he / she / it? | He's / She's / It's 5 (years old). |
| | are you / we/ they? | You're / We're / They're 42. |

**3** Correct the mistake in each sentence.

1 How old he is?
2 I have 22 years old.
3 She's 18 years.
4 They haven't 40.

## Possessive adjectives / Possessive ('s) → 2C

| Subject | | Possessive | |
|---|---|---|---|
| I | work here. This is | my | office. |
| You | 're Zac, right? What's | your | surname? |
| Jack (He) | loves | his | new job. |
| Ms Fox (She) | isn't at work today. | Her | car isn't here. |
| New York (It) | 's a fantastic city! | Its | shops are great! |
| We | don't have a dog. | Our | pet's a cat. |
| Ed & Di (They) | love dogs. They're | their | favourite animals. |

| | |
|---|---|
| This is Jack's office. | This is his office. |
| That's Ms Fox's car. | That's her car. |
| What's the cat's name? | What's its name? |
| That's Ed and Di's dog. | That's their dog. |

**4** Circle the right answer.

1 John's book = *possession / the verb be.*
2 John's a teacher = *possession / the verb be.*
3 Possessive adjectives *have / don't have* a plural form *(our book / our books).*
4 Use *her* for a *man / woman.*
5 Use *his* for a *man / woman.*
6 Use *your* for *a woman only / a man or a woman.*
7 English has *seven / eight* possessive adjectives.
8 *You* singular and *you* plural have *the same / a different* possessive adjective.

**5** Rewrite the sentence using an apostrophe *'s*.

1 It's the charity of Elton John. *It's Elton John's charity.*

2 He's the husband of Angelina. ______

3 She's the sister of Madonna. ______

4 They're the friends of Cameron Diaz. ______

5 It's a restaurant of McDonald. ______

**6** Replace the names in Exercise 5 with possessive adjectives.

1 *Elton John's= his*

2 ______

3 ______

4 ______

5 ______

## Present simple: I, you, we, they → 2D, 2E

| *Wh–* Questions | | | |
|---|---|---|---|
| Where | do | you we they | live? work? |
| What | | | do? |
| What languages | | | speak? |

| Positive | | Negative | | |
|---|---|---|---|---|
| I You We They | live ... work ... have ... speak ... | I You We They | don't | live ... work ... have ... speak ... |

| Question | | | Short answers | | |
|---|---|---|---|---|---|
| Do | I you we they | live ...? work ...? have ...? speak ...? play ...? | Yes, | you I we they | do. |
| | | | No, | | don't. |

**7** Complete the rules with *do*, *don't* or *verb*.

1 To make questions with *I*, *you*, *we* and *they*, you need *do* + a ______.

2 Word order in questions = *do* + subject + ______.

3 Use ______ + verb to make negatives.

4 Positive, negative and question ______ forms are the same for *I*, *you*, *we* and *they*.

5 Short answers are *Yes, I* ______ or *No, I* ______.

**8** Complete the table.

| Positive | Negative |
|---|---|
| They work a lot. | *They don't work a lot.* |
| We have two sons. | ______ |
| You speak French. | ______ |
| ______ | I don't like it. |
| They smoke. | ______ |
| ______ | We don't buy cigarettes. |
| ______ | I don't understand this. |

**9** Write your questions. Then write your short answers.

1 *Do you play tennis?*

2 Italian? ______?

3 ______?

4 ______?

5 ______?

**1** on on in on at in in at
**2** 1 CAPITAL M T W 2 small m a n 3 CAPITAL C J R 4 CAPITAL L R O S
**3** 2 I am 22 years old. 3 She's 18. 4 They aren't 40.
**4** 1 possession 2 *be* 3 don't have 4 woman 5 man
6 a man or a woman 7 seven 8 the same
**5** 2 He's Angelina's husband. 3 She's Madonna's sister.
4 They're Cameron Diaz's friends. 5 It's a McDonald's restaurant.
**6** 2 her 3 her 4 their 5 their
**7** 1 verb 2 verb 3 don't 4 verb 5 do, don't
**8** We don't have two sons. You don't speak French. I like it. They don't smoke. We buy cigarettes. I understand this.
**9** 2 Do you speak Italian? 3 Do you have a car? 4 Do you play (like) football? 5 Do you have a cat?

# 3 Essential Grammar

## Suggestions: *Let's* + verb → 3A

| | ⊕ | ⊖ |
|---|---|---|
| Let's have dinner together. | Sure.<br>That's a good idea!<br>OK, why not? | Sorry, I can't.<br>I'm busy. |

## Requests: *Can I use ...? Can you ...?* → 3A

| | | | |
|---|---|---|---|
| Can I | use | your pen, please | ⊕ Yes, of course.<br>Here you are.<br>Certainly.<br>Sure. |
| Can you | lend me | | ⊖ No, sorry.<br>Sorry, I don't have ... |

**1** Write (T) true or (F) false.

1 *Let's* is a contraction of *let us* and is a plural form. T
2 *Can/can't* has one positive and one negative form for all persons. ___
3 To make requests, use *Can* + verb + pronoun. ___
4 Use 'sorry' when you say *Yes*. ___
5 *Can* also means *I (don't) know how to*. For example, *I can swim* or *I can't swim*. ___

**2** Order the words to make suggestions or requests and add a word from the box.

go lend ~~open~~ stay use

1 window Can the please window I ? *Can I open the window please?*
2 tonight out Let's ______
3 your please you Can car us ? ______
4 we Can your computer? ______
5 watch home TV at and Let's . ______

**3** Match the answers, a–e to 1–5.

a No, sorry, I'm tired today. ☐
b No, sorry, I need it to go to work. ☐
c That's a good idea? What's on? ☐
d Yes, of course. It's hot today, isn't it? 1
e Sure. Here you are. It's a PC. Is that OK? ☐

## Present simple: he, she, it → 3B, 3C, 3D, 3E, 4A

| Positive | | Negative | | |
|---|---|---|---|---|
| Leo<br>Anna | lives ...<br>has ...<br>speaks ... | He<br>She | doesn't | live ...<br>have ...<br>speak ... |
| The show | starts ... | It | | start ... |

| Questions | | | Short answers | | |
|---|---|---|---|---|---|
| Does | Leo<br>Anna | live ...?<br>have ...?<br>speak ...? | Yes, | he<br>she<br>it | does. |
| | it | start ...? | No, | | doesn't. |

| *Wh-* Questions | | | |
|---|---|---|---|
| Where | does | Leo<br>Anna<br>he<br>she | live? |
| What | | | do on Fridays? |
| What languages | | | speak? |
| What time | | it | start? |

**4** Complete the rules with the words in the box.

does doesn't s everyday verb

1 *He*, *she* and *it* forms always end with the letter __.
2 Use ______ + subject + verb to make questions with *he*, *she* and *it*.
3 Use *doesn't* + ______ to make negatives.
4 Short answers end in *does* or ______.
5 Use the present simple for ______ activities.
6 The negative of *My sister has a car* is *My sister* ______ *have a car*. The question is ______ *she have a car?*
7 Be careful with the spelling of *go*: *I go* but *He goe*__.

**5** Complete the table.

| I | he, she |
|---|---|
| live | *lives* |
| have | ______ |
| do | ______ |
| ______ | goes |
| drive | ______ |
| play | ______ |
| study | ______ |
| work | ______ |

**6** Complete the questions. Use the correct verb from Exercise 5. Then write the answers. Use the information in brackets.

1 *Does* Al *work* in L.A? (yes, actor) — 1 *Yes, he does. He's an actor.*
2 ______ Al ______ to work every day? (No, five days a week) — 2 ______
3 ______ Al ______ in a flat? (No, house) — 3 ______
4 ______ Al ______ Spanish? (Yes, speak very well) — 4 ______
5 ______ Al ______ children? (No, alone) — 5 ______
6 ______ Al ______ tennis? (No, football) — 6 ______

## Prepositions of time → 3D, 3E

My friend Al:
- wakes up **at** 6:30.
  He leaves home **at about** 8 o'clock.
  He doesn't have lunch **before** 2 p.m.
  He has dinner **after** 8.

**7** Read about Al and tick (✓) the false picture.

## Adverbs of frequency → 3F

100%

| | |
|---|---|
| always | Carla's **always** late for work. |
| usually | She **hardly ever** leaves home before 9:30, |
| often | She **often** gets to work after 10! |
| sometimes | She's **never** there when you need her! |
| hardly ever | |
| never | |

0%

**8** Complete the rule with *before* or *after*.

Adverbs of frequency go ______ the verb *be* and ______ all other verbs.

**9** Put the adverbs in the box in the correct place in the sentences.

always never often usually ~~usually~~

1 Carla *usually* leaves home after 9.30 in the morning.
2 Carla arrives at work on time.
3 She doesn't get there before 10 a.m.
4 She arrives after 10 in the morning.
5 She is in the wrong place when you need her!

**1** 2 T 3 F 4 F 5 T
**2** 2 Let's go out tonight. 3 Can you lend us your car, please? 4 Can we use your computer? 5 Let's stay at home and watch TV.
**3** a 2 b 3 c 5 d 1 e 4 **4** 1 s 2 does 3 verb 4 doesn't 5 everyday 6 doesn't, Does 7 s
**5** has does go drives plays studies works
**6** 2 Does go 3 Does live 4 Does speak 5 Does have 6 Does play
2 No, he doesn't. He goes to work five days a week. 3 No, he doesn't. He lives in a house. 4 Yes, he does. He speaks very well.
5 No, he doesn't. He lives alone. 6 No, he doesn't. He plays football.
**7** 3 false **8** after, before **9** 2 Carla never arrives at 3 She doesn't often 4 She usually arrives 5 She is always in

# 4 Essential Grammar

## Dates → 4B

| | | |
|---|---|---|
| When's | your<br>his<br>her<br>their<br>Sam's | birthday? |
| What day is it today? | | |
| What's the date today? | | |

| | | |
|---|---|---|
| It's | on | Friday.<br>7th August.<br>the 14th. |
| | in | May. |
| | Wednesday. | |
| | 11th November. | |

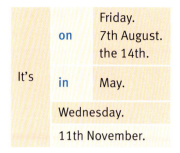

*My birthday's on the twenty-ninth of February but I usually celebrate on March the first.*

**1** Circle the correct answer.

1 Use *in / on* + days.

2 Use *in / on* + months when you don't say the date.

3 When you say a date, *say / don't say* 'the'.

**2** Complete the sentence with *in*, *on* or Ø.

*It's Jo's birthday ...* Ø soon.

___ Monday. ___ today. ___ next Monday.

___ July 4th. ___ June. ___ the 4th of July.

## Object pronouns → 4C

| | | Subject | | Object |
|---|---|---|---|---|
| | Does | she | like | me? |
| A | | I | love | you. |
| B | | We | don't know | him. |
| C | | He | works with | her. |
| D | | They | hate | it! |
| E | I think | it's | perfect for | us. |
| F | Do | you | remember | them? |

**3** Which of these sentences go before A–F in the table?

1 Anna and Leo at the opera? No way! D

2 Look at this computer, Sam. ☐

3 Do you know this man? ☐

4 Look! Guns n Roses are on TV. ☐

5 Bill knows Sue very well. ☐

6 Do you like me or love me? ☐

**4** Complete the rules with pronouns from the table.

1 Use he and him → singular, for a man.

2 Use ____ and ____ → singular, for a woman

3 One subject and object pronoun has the same form → ____.

4 Use ____ → singular, for a thing or an animal.

5 Use ____ and ____ → plural, for people, things or animals.

6 ____ and ____ = *you* + *I* and *you* + *me*.

**5** Answer the question with *Yes, I really love* or *No I really hate* + an object pronoun.

Do you like...

1 ... U2? No, I really hate them.

2 ... apples? Yes, I really love ______

3 ... skiing? ______

4 ... pasta? ______

5 ... Madonna? ______

6 ... small dogs? ______

7 ... Bruce Willis? ______

8 ... beer? ______

**1** 1 on 2 in 3 say
**2** on on 0 in 0 on
**3** 2 E 3 B 4 F 5 C 6 A
**4** 2 she/her 3 you 4 it 5 they/them 6 we/us
**5** 2 them 3 it 4 it 5 her 6 them 7 him 8 it
**6** 1 ing 2 e, ing 3 consonant, consonant 4 ing
**7** 1 smoking 2 dancing 3 watching 4 chatting
5 talking 6 studying 7 having 8 E-mailing
**8** 2 How often do you play the piano?
3 How often do you play football?
4 How often do you do yoga?
5 How often do you go running?
a 2 b other 5 c a 3 d twice 1 e times 4
**9** 1 go 2 play 3 do 4 Go 5 Do 6 Play

## Verb+*ing* → 4D

| | | | | | |
|---|---|---|---|---|---|
| I<br>You<br>We<br>They | like<br>don't like<br>hate<br>prefer | walking.<br>dancing.<br>running. | Running<br>Walking | is | excellent exercise.<br>very relaxing. |
| He<br>She<br>It | likes<br>doesn't like<br>loves | | | | |

| Spelling of *-ing* form | | |
|---|---|---|
| go<br>read | + *ing* | going<br>reading |
| drive<br>write | – ***e*** + *ing* | driving<br>writing |
| sit<br>swim | + ***t*** + *ing*<br>+ ***m*** + *ing* | sitting<br>swimming |

**6** Complete the rules with these words or letters.

-ing    e    consonant

1 Add ____________ to verbs to make activities. (work**ing**, eat**ing**)

2 For verbs ending in ___, cut the ____________ and add ____________. (tak**ing**, liv**ing**)

3 For one-syllable verbs ending vowel + ____________, double the ____________. (sit**ting**, stop**ping**)

4 After *love*, *prefer*, *like* and *hate*, use verb + ____________ (I love sleep**ing**).

**7** Correct one mistake in each sentence.

1 I hate smokeing.
2 Lu loves dance.
3 Cal prefers watch TV.
4 Do you like chating online?
5 Talk on MSN is easy.
6 Study at weekends is boring!
7 I love have a shower before bed.
8 E-mail friends is a nice way to practise English.

## *How often …?* → 4E

| How often do you …? | | |
|---|---|---|
| Once<br>Twice<br>Three times<br>Every<br>Every<br>other | a | day.<br>week.<br>month.<br>year. |

## *play / go / do* → 4E

| | |
|---|---|
| play | golf |
| | tennis |
| | cards |
| go | skiing |
| | dancing |
| | cycling |
| do | yoga |
| | ballet |
| | martial arts |

**8** Ask *How often do you …?* for pictures 1–5. Complete the answers. Match them to a–e.

1 How often do you smoke? ____________
2 ____________
3 ____________
4 ____________
5 ____________

a Almost *every* night. I play in a band. ☐
b Every ________ day. I usually run about 6 kilometres in 30 minutes. ☐
c Once ________ week. In the park with my children. ☐
d Only ________ a day – one after lunch and one after dinner. ☐
e About three ________ week. I do it alone in my room for an hour. ☐

**9** Complete the rules and phrases with *play*, *go* or *do*.

1 Use ________ with activities (verb + *ing*).
2 Use ________ with games.
3 Use ________ with other physical activities.
4 ________ swimming, shopping and travelling.
5 ________ boxing, aerobics and karate.
6 ________ volleyball, rugby and baseball.

**Richmond Publishing**
4th Floor
26–28 Hammersmith Grove
London
W6 7BA

© Richmond Publishing, 2009

**ISBN:** 978-846-68-0598-8

*All rights reserved. No part of this book may be reproduced, stored in a retrieval system or transmitted in any form by any means, electronic, mechanical, photocopying, recording or otherwise, without the prior permission in writing of the publisher.*

Printed by Orymu, S.A.
D.L: M-10100-2009

**Project Development:** Sarah Thorpe
**Editors:** Lynda Parkinson, Virginia García
**Design and Layout:** Nigel Jordan, Phil Wilkes, Lorna Heaslip
**Cover Design:** Aqueduct, London and Richmond Publishing
**Photo Research:** Magdalena Mayo
**Audio Production:** Paul Ruben Productions, Inc. NYC

*Richmond Essential English Course* is an adaptation of *Interlink* (© Learning Factory, Ltda.)
Published under licence by Learning Factory Ltda.

The publishers would like to thank the original *Interlink* writing team:
Daniela Bertolucci, Carla Chaves, Angela Dias, Sebastião Ferreira, Lilian Lopes, Nelson Mitrano, Ricardo Sili, Rosane Thiebaut

*Every effort has been made to trace the holders of copyright before publication. The publishers will be pleased to rectify any error or omission at the earliest opportunity.*

**Illustrations:**
David Banks, Anne Cakebread, Andrew Hennessey, Matt Latchford, Marine, Gillian Martin

**Photographs:**
*A. Viñas; D. Lezama; E. Marín; GARCÍA-PELAYO/Juancho; J. A. Gutiérrez; J. Jaime; Krauel; M. Mayo; P. López; P. Vidal; S. Enríquez; T. Arias*; A. G. E. FOTOSTOCK; ALBUM/ WARNER BROS TV, LUCASFILM/JAK PRODUCTIONS, SONY PICTURES, GABRIEL SIMON PRODUCTION SERVICES/ STORYLINE ENTERTAINMENT/JAMES, DAVID, UNIVERSAL TV/20TH CENTURY FOX TV/KLASKY-SCUPO, WARNER BROTHERS, TOUCHSTONE PICTURES; CORDON PRESS/ Harpo Productions; COVER/CORBIS/Zefa/Gregor Schuster, Jim Craigmyle, Curtis/Strauss, Peter M. Fisher, EPA/Andy Rain, Zefa/H. Schmid, Tim Mosenfelder, Eye Ubiquitous/ Bryan Pickering, Envision/Steven Mark Needham, The Irish Image Collection; FOTOLIA/William Wang; FOTONONSTOP; GETTY IMAGES SALES SPAIN/Bongarts/Lars Baron, Taxi/ Doug Corrance, Stone/Roger Wright, Gustavo Caballero, Stone/Jutta Klee, Stone/Bob Thomas, Michael Buckner, Frazer Harrison, Frank Micelotta, Dilip Vishwanat, Ronald Martine, Johnny Franzen, Andrew Parsons, AFP/Robyn Beck, AFP/Jiji Press, Scott Barbour, Jeffrey Mayer, Evan Agostini, Chris Jackson, Peter Kramer, Chip Somodevilla, Martin Oeser, Bryan Bedder, FilmMagic/Charles Eshelman, Jack Hollingsworth, Vince Bucci, Kevin Casey, Stone/ Christopher Bissell, Photonica/Mark Horn, WireImage/ Ferdaus Shamim, Dave Hogan, WireImage/Jeffrey Mayer, BWP Media, WireImage/James Devaney, AFP/Toshifumi Kitamura, Taxi, Photonica/Meredith Heuer, Taxi/Caroline Schiff, Stone/Alex and Laila, WireImage/George Pimentel, WireImage/Mark Von Holden, ALLSPORT/Nick Wilson, Dorling Kindersley/Andy Crawford, Photographer's Choice/ Still Images, StockFood Creative/Bodo A. Schieren, Stone/ David Madison; HIGHRES PRESS STOCK/AbleStock. com; I. Preysler; ISTOCKPHOTO/Amy Dunn; MUSEUM ICONOGRAFÍA/*J. Martin*; PHOTODISC; SEIS X SEIS; STOCK PHOTOS; STOCKBYTE; Bank of Scotland Fireworks Concert, Edinburgh International Festival/Peter Sandground; Courtesy of the Festival International de Jazz de Montreal; Orchestra Giovanile 'Luigi Cherubini'; 2008 Marvel Characters, Inc.; European Community; FUJITSU/SIEMENS; MATTON-BILD; MUSEO EGIPCIO DE CHARLOTTENBURG, BERLÍN; Nokia Corporation; SERIDEC PHOTOIMAGENES CD; ARCHIVO SANTILLANA